1000+
of the best
BUCKET LIST
ideas

Published in the United States by Big Heart Books

BIG HEART
books

BRING YOUR BUCKET LIST TO LIFE WITH THE COMPANION PLANNING JOURNAL!

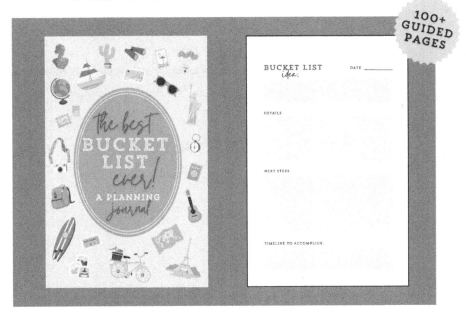

TURN YOUR DREAMS INTO REALITY!

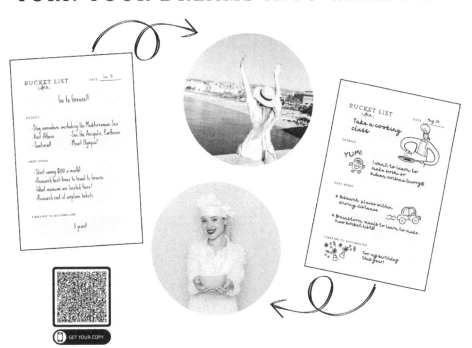

*"The biggest adventure you can ever take
is to live the life of your dreams."*
—OPRAH WINFREY

A bucket list is like a roadmap to the kind of life you've always dreamed about: It helps you steer the course of your life by making sure you accomplish the things that matter to you most.

That's what this entire book is devoted to: With more than one thousand ideas, it offers you the best ideas for creating your ultimate bucket list.

Those ideas are divided into more than 45 different themed lists, such as places made famous by pop-culture; thrill-seeking adventures to experience or creative endeavors to try. Thanks to this variety, you're sure to find those things that appeals to you the most as you create your ultimate bucket list.

And don't worry—we don't expect you to use all one thousand ideas! We suggest you bring a highlighter with you as you work through the book, marking your favorite ideas. Because your ultimate bucket list should be individually tailored to you and your interests!

(And if you need help collecting all those ideas into one place, check out this book's companion, **The Best Bucket List Ever!: A Planning Journal**, where you can write out all your top picks and flesh out plans to make those dreams a reality!)

Now, let the adventures begin!

100+ GUIDED JOURNAL PAGES TO HELP YOU PLAN YOUR *ultimate* BUCKET LIST!

TABLE OF CONTENTS

PART IV: OTHER BUCKET LIST IDEAS

CREATE YOUR OWN BUCKET LIST

PART I:

general Travel BUCKET LIST *ideas*

Travel is the most common item that people include on a bucket list. That shouldn't be much of a surprise, given that we live on a planet offering an incredible array of sights, sounds, tastes and cultures. Who wouldn't yearn to travel the globe and experience as much of it as possible?

That's why we've started our bucket list ideas here. The ideas in this section are more general, not necessarily tied to specific cities or locales. Instead, they can be incorporated almost anywhere and will help get your wheels turning about some of the travel basics that you want to incorporate into your bucket list:

What kind of trip do you want to plan? What kinds of adventures do you want to incorporate into it? What things do you want to see while you're there?

And that's just the beginning…

KINDS OF VACATIONS TO TAKE

Before you start marking up a map of places to go, we suggest starting at the beginning and thinking about the kind of trips you want to take. Because there's a big difference between staying at an all-inclusive, luxury resort and sleeping in a tent in the middle of nowhere. Consider these different vacation styles and accommodations:

- Hotel
- Bed & Breakfast
- Camping
- Glamping
- Tiny house
- Off-grid house
- Treehouse
- Yurt
- Log cabin
- Working farm
- Travel in a train
- Travel in an RV
- Backpacking
- Hostel
- Houseboat
- Yacht
- Windjammer cruise
- Riverboat cruise
- Ocean cruise
- Eco resort
- Amusement-park resort
- Casino resort
- Luxury resort

ADVENTURES TO GO ON

Now let's consider the kinds of adventures you'd like to experience on those trips. This list features more than two dozen of the best high-intensity, thrill-inducing activities you could incorporate into your bucket-list travels:

- Ziplining
- Hot-air balloon ride
- Skydiving from a plane
- Indoor skydiving
- Parasailing
- Hang gliding
- Surfing
- Jumping off a bridge
- Scuba diving
- Snorkeling
- Volcano boarding
- Bungee jumping
- Ride an ATV
- Skiing, snowboarding or snow tubing
- Take an ax-throwing class
- Snowmobiling
- Complete a tree-top adventure course
- Jet skiing
- White water rafting
- Canyoning
- Rock climbing
- Bouldering
- Windsurfing
- Barefoot water skiing

KINDS OF TRANSPORTATION TO RIDE IN

When you think of your bucket-list travels, how do you want to get around? This list will help you consider transports of all types, whether you want to take a spin in a souped-up hot rod, rent a tandem bike or check out some of the most unusual modes of transportation available around the world:

- Helicopter
- Tandem bicycle
- Limousine
- Motorcycle
- Scooter
- Classic antique car
- Convertible
- Hot rod
- Luxury car
- Horse-drawn carriage
- Subway
- Train
- Amtrak
- Glass-bottomed boat
- Paddle boat
- Ferry
- Houseboat
- Sailboat
- Yacht
- Catamaran
- Submarine
- Pirate ship cruise or tour
- A tap-tap in Haiti
- A jingle bus in Pakistan
- A double-decker bus in London
- A rickshaw in India
- A jeepney in Philippines
- A gondola in Venice
- An amphibious bus in the Netherlands
- A cable car in San Francisco
- The bullet train in Japan
- A swan boat in Boston Public Garden

THINGS TO SEE IN NATURE

Mother Nature is renowned for her diversity and originality—painting vistas of all colors, climates and curiosities. Here is a list of some of our favorite natural features that you might want to include in your bucket-list adventures:

- Cave
- Beach
- Rain forest
- Desert
- Safari
- Glacier
- Mountain
- Natural hot spring
- Coral reef
- Volcano
- Swamp
- Lagoon
- Wetlands
- Stream
- Alpine lake
- Meadow
- Visit both coasts
- Sand dunes
- Archipelago
- Fjord
- Deserted island
- Hug a redwood
- Visit a shipwreck
- Climb a lighthouse
- Hike the Appalachian Trail
- Sleep under the stars

VISIT THE SEVEN NATURAL WONDERS OF THE WORLD

If you could only see seven of the most breathtaking natural sites in the world, which ones would they be? CNN sought to answer that question, in collaboration with the Seven Natural Wonders organization, with the development of this list. (Notably, every inhabited continent has at least one site on the list.) Think of it like Mother Nature's "Best of" list:

Mount Everest, the highest point in the world, located in the Himalayan Mountains (China, Nepal)

Paricutín, a cinder cone volcano that abruptly rose out of a cornfield with its first eruptions in 1943 (Mexico)

The Grand Canyon, a massive, 277-mile-long gorge that stretches 4 to 18 miles wide and 1 mile deep, created by the Colorado River (Arizona)

Victoria Falls, a waterfall on the Zambezi River and one of the largest in the world, stretching more than 5,600 feet wide (Zambia, Zimbabwe)

Guanabara Bay, the largest bay in the world, it is majestically surrounded by mountains (Brazil)

Great Barrier Reef, the world's largest coral reef, stretching more than 133,000 square miles (Australia)

Northern Lights, known technically as the Aurora Borealis, are an unpredictable natural phenomenon caused when electrically-charged particles from solar storms collide with the Earth and get trapped at the earth's magnetic poles (various locations in the Arctic Circle, including Alaska)

ANIMAL ADVENTURES
TO EXPERIENCE

Are you an animal lover? Consider incorporating that interest into your bucket list with some of these ideas that will bring you up-close-and-personal with your favorite critters, or personalize them with provided fill-in-the-blank spots for some of them:

- Go to a zoo
- Go to a petting zoo
- Visit an animal sanctuary
- Visit a butterfly conservatory
- Visit an aquarium
- Go on a safari
- Visit an aviary
- Go to an insectarium
- Visit a birds of prey rehabilitation center
- Try goat yoga
- Hand-feed a _____ (bird, squirrel, some zoo animals)
- See a _____ (bald eagle, white tiger, lynx, moose)
- Hold a _____ (snake, tarantula, starfish)
- Ride a _____ (camel, horse, llama, elephant)
- Swim with _____ (dolphins, sharks, stingrays, sea turtles)
- Pet a _____ (shark, iguana, capybara, elephant, sloth)
- See manatees at **Crystal River,** considered the manatee capital of the world (Citrus County, Fla.)
- See bison roam at the **National Bison Range** (Charlo, Mont.)
- Observe grizzly bears and wolves at the **Grizzly & Wolf Discovery Center** (West Yellowstone, Mont.)

See the largest migrating elk heard in North America at **National Elk Refuge** (Jackson, Wyo.)

View the Monarch butterfly migration as millions of the orange butterflies overwinter at the **El Rosario Butterfly Sanctuary** (Michoacán, Mexico)

See wild ponies on **Assateague Island**, where they've lived for hundreds of years, after escaping a Spanish shipwreck (Assateague Island, Md.)

See flamingos in their natural habitat at the world's largest breeding colony of West Indian flamingos in **Inagua National Park** (Bahamas)

View sloths in the first facility dedicated solely to these animals at the **Sloth Sanctuary of Costa Rica** (Limón Province, Costa Rica)

Visit the world's largest puffin colony (Westman Islands, Iceland)

See pygmy hippos, which grow no larger than 3 feet tall, in one of their last remaining habitats (**Gola Rainforest National Park**, Sierra Leone and Liberia)

Visit the free-ranging colony of about 3,000 African penguins at **Boulders Beach** (Cape Town, South Africa)

Visit **Cat Island**, where several hundred cats run wild, having originally been imported to help control the island's mouse population (Tashirojima, Japan)

See more than 600 elephants at **Addo Elephant National Park** (Gqebera, South Africa)

See macaque monkeys warm up and play in **Hell's Valley** natural hot spring (Nagano, Japan)

THINGS TO DO ON A ROAD TRIP

Is there anything more classic than a cross-country road trip? That's why we've compiled this list of road trip-inspired ideas and pit-stops for any on-the-road adventure you might plan:

- Create a road-trip playlist for the drive
- Drive with the top down
- Sing along to a favorite song at the top of your lungs
- Navigate using old-school paper maps
- Play "I Spy"
- Play "20 Questions"
- Listen to a podcast
- Listen to an audiobook
- Stop at a famous landmark
- Collect postcards along the way
- Visit a public park
- Stop and pose with a sculpture
- Read a local newspaper
- Try a new-to-you local food along the way
- Check out a quirky roadside attraction
- Take a photo at a scenic overlook
- Stop at a state visitor center
- Collect brochures for interesting places
- Wave at a stranger in another car
- Do the "trucker's salute" (pumping your fist in the air) and get a semi-trunk to honk at you
- Find license plates from all 50 states
- Document the funniest or weirdest things you see along the way
- Listen to the local radio
- Call in to the local radio station and make a song request
- Stay at a bed-and-breakfast
- Eat at a greasy spoon
- Drive a scenic highway (see list, p. 39)

THINGS TO DO AT THE BEACH

Nothing says "vacation" like a trip to the beach. That's why we've compiled this list that pairs perfectly with any of the sun, sand and sea adventures that make your bucket list. (Now, just don't forget to pack the sunscreen!)

- Visit a beach in every color of sand: white, black, red, pink, orange, purple, gray and green
- Build a sandcastle
- Bury someone in the sand
- Witness a sand sculpting contest
- Watch the sunrise over the ocean
- Watch the sunset over the ocean
- Collect seashells
- See a jellyfish
- See a dolphin
- See a shark
- Find a piece of sea glass
- Find a piece of driftwood
- Have a picnic on the beach
- Sit under a beach umbrella
- Read a book in the sand
- Get a tan
- Eat ice cream
- Go ocean fishing
- Ride a boogie board
- Rent a beach cabana
- Play sand volleyball
- Rent a jet ski
- Do beach yoga
- Send a message in a bottle
- Dig for buried treasure
- Walk the boardwalk or pier
- Write your name in the sand
- Float in an inflatable

THINGS TO DO WHILE CAMPING

Camping is practically a rite of passage, ushering us away from the distractions of modern, everyday life and drawing us into the splendor and serenity of nature. Soak it all up with these ideas for an unforgettable, bucket-list camping excursion:

- Cook over an open fire
- Roast marshmallows
- Make s'mores
- Sleep in a sleeping bag
- Pitch a tent
- Look for a shooting star
- Tell scary ghost stories
- Build a fire
- Build a fire without matches
- Relax in a hammock
- Catch fireflies
- Stargaze
- Find a waterfall
- Catch a fish
- Look for animal tracks
- Eat trail mix
- Make hot chocolate or coffee over the campfire
- Sleep under the stars
- Hike a trail
- Skip rocks at a creek or lake

THINGS TO DO
WHILE IN THE MOUNTAINS

Naturalist John Muir famously said, "The mountains are calling, and I must go." Many have followed in his footsteps and flocked to high peaks, whether it's for a sense of adventure, tranquility, inspiration, or even spiritual enlightenment. Given that there are over a million mountains on Earth, it shouldn't be too hard to make this bucket-list item happen with help from these ideas:

- Hike to the summit of a mountain
- Take a selfie at the peak
- Camp under the stars
- Go mountain biking
- Explore a mountain town
- Try rock climbing
- Attend a mountain festival
- Go fly fishing
- Take a sunrise hike
- Learn to use a map and compass for navigation
- Join a guided nature walk
- Learn mountain survival skills
- Create and decorate your own walking stick
- Create your own storytelling stick
- Research ahead of time the animals that can be seen where you'll be visiting
- Document the various wildlife you encounter
- Buy local art or artisan crafts
- Go mushroom hunting
- Wade into a mountain stream or lake
- Hike trails with different difficulty levels
- Check out the ranger- or visitor-center of a park
- Pan for gold (check local laws)
- Go gemstone or fossil mining (check local laws)

THINGS IN THE COSMOS
TO SEE THAT ARE
OUT OF THIS WORLD!

Sometimes the most beautiful sights are right before us. Or, right above us. In the modern world, we often forget that and ignore the celestial wonders right overhead. Make it a point to remedy that with some of these bucket-list experiences:

- See a solar eclipse
- See a lunar eclipse
- Watch a meteor shower and see shooting stars
- View the Milky Way
- See the North Star (Polaris)
- See the brightest star, Sirius
- Locate a constellation, such as the Big Dipper
- See Venus in the night sky
- See Mars in the night sky
- See Jupiter in the night sky
- Witness Halley's Comet (it passes by the Earth every 76 years, so it will next appear in 2062)
- Witness the Northern Lights
- Learn celestial navigation

PART II

United States Travel BUCKET LIST ideas

According to the World Atlas, only Russia and Canada are bigger than the United States. So it makes sense that any bucket list would make it a point to explore and experience all this country has to offer—which, trust us, is a lot!

VISIT ALL 50 STATES

50 states offer ample opportunities for adventures and sightseeing adventures of all kinds! Consider making it a point to visit states that you have never visited:

- Alabama
- Alaska
- Arizona
- Arkansas
- California
- Colorado
- Connecticut
- Delaware
- Florida
- Georgia
- Hawaii
- Idaho
- Illinois
- Indiana
- Iowa
- Kansas
- Kentucky
- Louisiana
- Maine
- Maryland
- Massachusetts
- Michigan
- Minnesota
- Mississippi
- Missouri

- Montana
- Nebraska
- Nevada
- New Hampshire
- New Jersey
- New Mexico
- New York
- North Carolina
- North Dakota
- Ohio
- Oklahoma
- Oregon
- Pennsylvania
- Rhode Island
- South Carolina
- South Dakota
- Tennessee
- Texas
- Utah
- Vermont
- Virginia
- Washington
- West Virginia
- Wisconsin
- Wyoming

TOP TOURIST CITIES
TO VISIT IN THE U.S.

This list looks at the No. 1 cities that people visit in the United States each year. Because if everyone else is doing it, there's a probably a good reason why. Read on for those cities and some of their top attractions:

New York City, iconic landmarks include Times Square, Central Park, the Statue of Liberty as well as world-class museums, Broadway shows, and diverse neighborhoods full of history

Miami, known for its South Beach nightlife, Little Havana cuisine and art deco architecture along Ocean Drive, it is a hotspot for fashion, art, and international flair

Orlando, featuring multiple world-renowned theme parks, it's known as the theme park capital of the world, but also offers year-round beach weather that visitors enjoy

Los Angeles, the entertainment capital of the world, it's where you'll find Hollywood but also Santa Monica Pier, Venice Beach, and the chic shopping of Rodeo Drive

San Francisco, where you can ride historic cable cars, explore neighborhoods like Haight-Ashbury, visit Alcatraz Island, and savor seafood at Fisherman's Wharf

Las Vegas, a desert oasis, the town is known for its over-the-top casinos and resorts as well as its world-class shows and entertainment

Washington, D.C., the nation's capital, it is like a living history book filled with monuments, museums, and historic memorials

Chicago, known for its deep-dish pizza, Navy Pier and Millennium Park, it even has a beach along Lake Michigan as well as iconic skyscrapers, including the former Sears Tower

Boston, where you'll find historic sites like the Freedom Trail and Paul Revere's House, it's also home to Boston Common, Harvard University and the Museum of Fine Arts

Honolulu, it's a tropic paradise with Waikiki Beach and Diamond Head also offering traditional luaus, snorkeling, whale-watching and more

Seattle, known not only for its coffee (as the birthplace of Starbucks) but also for its giant Ferris wheel, boat ferries and its original Pioneer Square with underground tours

San Diego, features a historic Gaslamp Quarter, the world-renowned San Diego Zoo, Balboa Park, and sunny beaches including La Jolla and Coronado

Atlanta, this sprawling metropolis offers history, with the Martin Luther King Jr. National Historic Site, as well as the Atlanta Botanical Garden and High Museum of Art

Key West, the southernmost point of the continental U.S., it's known for its vibrant nightlife, picturesque beaches, coral reefs, and water sports

OTHER CITIES
WORTH EXPLORING
IN THE U.S.

Let's be honest from the get-go: This list is not exhaustive. There are hundreds of cities in the U.S. that are hidden jewels for vacationers. So, consider these a jumping-off point as you craft your bucket list and consider unexpected places for your journeys:

Savannah, Ga., Spanish moss hangs from trees in this historic town renowned for its beauty that inspired General Sherman to offer the city as a gift to President Lincoln during the Civil War

Salem, Mass., home of the historic Salem Witch Trials in 1692-1693, during which more than 200 people were accused of being witches and 30 people executed

Mackinac Island, Mich., located in Lake Huron, cars are prohibited on the island so plan to rent a bike and indulge in the island's famous fudge

Charleston, S.C., with cobblestone streets and antebellum architecture, it's rife with historic plantations, Lowcountry cuisine, and is home to Rainbow Row, the nation's longest continuous row of Georgian-style houses

Minneapolis, one of the "Twin Cities," overlooks the Mississippi River and is a testament to the beauty of the outdoors with multiple parks and reserves sprinkled throughout the city as well as a vibrant and renowned arts scene

Dallas, points of interest include the iconic Nasher Sculpture Center, the site of the JFK assassination, it is also home to the Texas State Fair as well as a healthy mix of history, art, music, and food attractions

Birmingham, Ala., this city got its start with the rise of steel and iron industries, which are still celebrated in one of its most notable icons, the cast-iron Vulcan statue atop Red Mountain; also enjoy Southern cooking, outdoors and various historic sites, including from the Civil Rights Era

Bar Harbor, Maine, a haven for outdoor enthusiasts with hiking trails and whale-watching excursions, it is the gateway to Acadia National Park and known for its seafood

Austin, Texas, considered the "Live Music Capital of the World," it also is home to the Driskill, Mount Bonnell and a large natural spring-fed public swimming pool

Memphis, Tenn., situated along the Mississippi River, it is considered the birthplace of blues music and is known also for its Southern cuisine

Sedona, Ariz., nestled amid red rock formations, the town is known for its Tlaquepaque Arts & Crafts Village, scenic hikes like Cathedral Rock, as well as being a vortex site for spiritual seekers

Colorado Springs, Colo., straddling the Colorado Rockies and the Great Plains, feature attractions include Garden of the Gods, Pikes Peak Cog Railway, and U.S. Olympic & Paralympic Museum

Gatlinburg, Tenn., a charming mountain resort town offering plenty of options for nature-lovers and entertainment-seekers alike, it is known as the Gateway to the Smokey Mountains

Big Sur, Calif., this coastal town offers gorgeous scenery at multiple state parks, beaches and even just off the side of the road

St. Louis, Mo., along Route 66 and along the Mississippi River, this city is home to the Gateway Arch, a zoo (with free admission!), and multiple museums (science, history, art, architecture and more)

New Orleans, nicknamed the "Big Easy," this Mississippi River town is known for its Cajun cooking and culture, vibrant entertainment and historic, old-world charm, top spots include Bourbon Street, the Riverwalk, and St. Louis Cathedral

Nashville, Tenn., the state capital and home to Vanderbilt University, it is the celebrated center for country music but also pays homage to multiple presidents, museums and even a replica of the Parthenon in Greece

ICONIC SITES TO VISIT IN THE U.S.

You know those vintage postcards that invariably say things like, "Wish you were here!"? They almost always feature some kind of recognizable landmark or notable attraction. This list is kind of like that: a collection of the top iconic sites to visit around the country. (Maybe even grab a postcard while you're there!)

Golden Gate Bridge, spanning 1.7 miles it has been an iconic San Francisco landmark since it was built in 1933 (San Francisco)

The Hollywood sign, erected in 1923, it is an icon of Hollywood Hills and originally read "Hollywoodland," advertising a (then) new real estate neighborhood (Los Angeles)

The Hollywood Walk of Fame, located in the sidewalk along Hollywood Boulevard, more than 2,600 brass stars honor various entertainment legends, including Marilyn Monroe and Michael Jackson (Los Angeles)

Times Square, a cultural hub of theaters, music halls and upscale hotels, it is located at the intersection of Broadway, Seventh Avenue and 42nd Street in Midtown Manhattan (New York)

The White House, home of the President, it is open for free tours year-round, though tickets must be requested in advance (Washington, D.C.)

Grand Ole Opry, launched in 1925 with a barn dance, the building is now a country music mecca where legendary musicians still perform (Nashville, Tenn.)

Space Needle, Seattle's skyline gem, offers panoramic views of the city, nearby mountains and Puget Sound (Seattle)

Gateway Arch, take an elevator ride for breathtaking views overlooking the Mississippi River, at 630 feet high, it is the tallest monument in the country (St. Louis)

Biltmore Estate, built in 1895 by the Vanderbilt family, the elaborate home sits on 8,000 acres in the Blue Ridge mountains, making it America's largest privately-owned house (Asheville, N.C.)

LOVE sculpture, created by Robert Indiana in 1970, it has been a global symbol of love ever since—fitting given Philadelphia is known as a the City of Brotherly Love (Philadelphia)

Harvard University, founded in 1636, it is the nation's oldest university and its most prestigious Ivy League institution (Cambridge, Mass.)

Central Park, designed in 1858, it is an 843-acre oasis in the middle of the city, complete with formal gardens, winding sidewalks, multiple lakes, a castle and even a zoo! (New York)

Brooklyn Bridge, this iconic suspension bridge was considered a feat of engineering when it was constructed in 1883, connecting the boroughs of Manhattan and Brooklyn (New York)

Fallingwater, built over a waterfall in 1935 by renowned architect Frank Lloyd Wright, it is considered a masterpiece of modern architecture (Mill Run, Pa.)

The French Quarter, founded in 1718, experience the historic heart of the city through its unique Creole cuisine, jazz music and nightlife (New Orleans)

Pike Place Market, originally opened in 1907, this iconic market overlooks Puget Sound where you can buy fresh fish, produce and more (Seattle)

■ **Las Vegas Strip**, a famous entertainment hub of upscale casino hotels offering world-class shows for music, comedy and circus-style acts under glittering lights (Las Vegas)

■ **Billy Bob's**, the world's largest honky-tonk, it was established in 1981 and is an iconic country music venue (Fort Worth, Texas)

■ **Sun Valley**, America's oldest ski resort, it's famous for its Nordic skiing as well as various outdoor adventure, music and arts opportunities (Sun Valley, Idaho)

■ **Skydeck Chicago at Willis Tower**, the highest observation deck in the country, at 110 stories and 1,451 feet high (Chicago)

■ **Millennium Park**, home of the sculpture known as "the Bean," it is also one of the largest green roofs in the world and the city's second most-visited tourist attraction (Chicago)

■ **Mall of America**, with more than 500 stores and 96 acres big, it is the country's largest mall, complete with an aquarium and indoor amusement park (Bloomington, Minn.)

ICONIC NATURAL SITES TO VISIT IN THE U.S.

There's a reason they call it "America the Beautiful." From sea to shining sea, you'll find lakes, rivers, wetlands, desert, prairies, canyons, and purple mountains majesties. Why not add some of these most iconic natural beauties to your bucket list and see for yourself what all the fuss is about:

Visit a National Park (see list, p. 36)

Niagara Falls, one of the most famous waterfalls in the world, where more than 3,000 tons of water flow over the falls every second (Niagara Falls, N.Y.)

The Grand Canyon, a massive, 277-mile-long gorge that stretches 4 to 18 miles wide and 1 mile deep, created by the Colorado River (Arizona)

Hoover Dam, called an engineering marvel, it is a 276-foot-tall dam built during the Great Depression to tame the Colorado River (Nevada)

The Mississippi River, the world's fourth-longest river spanning more than 2,300 miles cutting through the center of the country, it has been a historically crucial waterway for travel, commerce and agriculture (various)

Pikes Peak, part of the Rocky Mountains, it is known as "America's Mountain" and inspired the song "America the Beautiful" (Colorado Springs, Colo.)

Lake Michigan, its shores provide the largest freshwater sand dunes in the world that make for freshwater beaches (Mich., Ill., Wis.)

Lake Erie, supposedly it is home to its own Loch Ness-like sea monster, affectionately known as "Bessie" and has had more than 2,000 shipwrecks, though only 375 have been found (Ohio, Pa., N.Y.)

Great Salt Lake, the largest saltwater lake in the Western Hemisphere, it is the remnant of an ancient lake from the Ice Age and is too salty to support fish and most aquatic life (Utah)

Antelope Canyon, famous for its slot canyons and narrow passages that make for breathtaking photos, it was carved by flash floods and wind erosion over millions of years (Page, Arizona)

Valley of Fire State Park, these red rock formations appear to be "on fire" when illuminated by the sun and date back over 150 million years (Moapa Valley, Nevada)

Glenwood Springs, home of the largest mineral hot springs pool in the world, it is renowned for its therapeutic properties and surrounding mountain vista (Glenwood Springs, Colo.)

Shoshone Falls, called the Niagara of the West, the Snake River plunges over a 212-foot-tall cliff here (Twin Falls, Idaho)

Hells Canyon, North America's deepest river gorge is almost 2,000 feet deeper than the Grand Canyon; look for Native American pictographs on canyon walls and wildlife like mountain goats and bighorn sheep (Hells Canyon, Idaho)

Devils Tower National Monument, the country's first national monument, it is a unique butte of lava that rises 867 feet into the sky—serving as a destination for rock climbers as well as a sacred location for many Native American tribes (Devils Tower, Wyo.)

"Tulip City, USA," where more than 6 million tulips bloom each spring (Holland, Mich.)

Pictured Rocks National Lakeshore, the country's first national seashore, it is named for the brightly colored sandstone cliffs that can be witnessed here (Munising, Mich.)

Minnehaha Regional Park, features Minnehaha Falls, a 53-foot waterfall that's breathtaking when they freeze during the winter (Minneapolis)

Mt. St. Helens, an active stratovolcano in the Pacific Northwest, it's most famous for its major eruption in 1980, which drastically reshaped the landscape (Toutle, Wash.)

VISIT A NATIONAL PARK

Ever since 1862 when the first National Park was established with Yellowstone National Park, the National Park system has attracted millions of visitors. In total, 63 National Parks are designated throughout the United States, encompassing 85 million acres and covering 3.4 percent of the total United States. Needless to say, they offer plenty of opportunities to experience Mother Nature! Read on for some of our favorite ones to visit around the country and why:

Acadia National Park, situated on Mount Desert Island, you can climb Champlain Mountain and visit sandy beaches (Maine)

Everglades National Park, the country's largest subtropical wilderness, is the natural, swampy habitat for animals including the manatee, American crocodile, and the elusive Florida panther (Florida)

Great Smoky Mountains National Park, breathtaking views of the Smoky Mountains it includes more than 800 miles of hiking trails (Tennessee, North Carolina)

Mammoth Cave National Park, the world's longest known cave system, it features massive chambers, huge underground cathedrals, as well as underground rivers (Kentucky)

Shenandoah National Park, located in the Appalachian Mountains, it is known for its 105-mile-long, overlook Skyline Drive, cascading waterfalls, springtime wildflowers and more (Virginia)

Petrified Forest National Park, it is in the Painted Desert and features trees that grew 200 million years ago that have now been fossilized (Arizona)

Arches National Park, the landscape is studded with more than 2,000 naturally arch-shaped, sandstone structures that look like something out of a Dali painting (Utah)

Bryce Canyon National Park, here you'll find one of the world's most extensive collections of "hoodoos," tall, rock pillars resulting from erosion (Utah)

Crater Lake National Park, the nation's deepest lake that's the result of a volcanic eruption 8,000 years ago; it is also one of the world's clearest lakes, with its water coming almost entirely from snow and rainfall (Oregon)

Grand Teton National Park, featuring the snow-capped Teton Mountains that overlook Jackson Hole Valley and the Jenny and Jackson lakes below; adjoins Yellowstone (Wyoming)

Hawaii Volcanoes National Park, visit two of the world's most active volcanoes (Hawaii)

Joshua Tree National Park, where the Mojave and Colorado deserts meet, this park provides picturesque vistas of cacti and is popular for camping (California)

Olympic National Park, includes the Hoh Rainforest, Mount Storm King, the Hall of Mosses as well as 70 miles of Pacific Northwest coastline (Washington)

Rocky Mountain National Park, check out all that the Rockies have to offer, including scenic trails for hiking, lakes as well as mountains, all in one park (Colorado)

Sequoia National Park, boasts the largest trees in the world, where you can see the General Sherman Tree that measures 275 feet tall and more than 36 feet in diameter (California)

Yellowstone National Park, the country's first National Park, it features multiple hot springs and geysers, including Old Faithful (Wyoming, Montana, Idaho)

Yosemite National Park, features notable waterfalls such as Vernal and Bridalveil Falls and Half Dome and El Capitan granite formations (California)

Zion National Park, featuring Zion Canyon and Virgin River, activities here can include canyoneering, rock climbing, horseback riding and more (Utah)

Denali National Park, boasts the highest peak in North America (Alaska)

Glacier Bay National Park, a favorite destination for cruise ships, you can spot glaciers and a variety of ocean life, including humpback whales (Alaska)

Katmai National Park, its giant Brooks Falls is famous for its salmon in summer and, subsequently, hungry brown bears (Alaska)

Wrangell-St. Elias National Park, the largest national park in the U.S., where you can check out glaciers that cover more than one-third of the park (Alaska)

You can purchase an annual park pass (currently $80) or visit the parks on one of their "Free Entrance Days," which take place throughout the year on certain holidays, such as Juneteenth, Veterans Day and the first day of National Park Week. (Visit nps.gov for more details.)

FAMOUS SCENIC HIGHWAYS
TO DRIVE IN THE U.S.

It's been said, "The road less travelled is the road to adventure." Which is why we're such fans of scenic highways —roads that have been specifically designated for having exceptional natural, historic or archaeological significance— even if it takes a little bit longer. Which road will you take?

Pacific Coast Highway or **California's Route 1**, stretches along the California coastline, taking you through Big Sur, multiple state parks and many beaches

Road to Hana, 55-miles long, it begins in Kahului, Hawaii and ends in the rustic village of Hana where you'll find black-sand beaches

Historic Columbia River Highway, the nation's first planned scenic road passes by multiple waterfalls, including Multnomah Falls, along the Columbia Gorge in Oregon

Route 66, called "the Mother Road" that once connected Chicago and Los Angeles, it remains a tribute to vintage Americana

Black Bear Scenic Byway, this stretch from Silver Springs to the Atlantic Coast takes you through the heart of Florida's Ocala National Forest

Lamoille Canyon Scenic Byway, a 12-mile drive through Humboldt National Forest takes you along a glacier-carved canyon in the Ruby Mountains of Nevada

Overseas Highway, the only road connecting the Florida Keys, it stretches 107 miles between the islands over the Atlantic Ocean and Gulf of Mexico

Blue Ridge Parkway, connecting Shenandoah National Park in Virginia and the Great Smokey Mountains Park in

North Carolina, it winds 450 miles through the Appalachian Mountains

Turquoise Trail, running through New Mexico, it is named for the turquoise gemstone mined in the area and takes travelers up Sandia Crest, which overlooks Albuquerque and Rio Grande Valley

Beartooth Highway, winding through the Rocky Mountains and past Yellowstone National Park, it reaches close to 11,000 feet in elevation

The Grand Circle, it winds through five states and nine national parks through the Southwest, including Zion National Park and the Grand Canyon as well as Las Vegas

Maine's Route 1, more than 500 miles long, this highway follows Maine's coastline through rustic seaside towns, Acadia National Park and more

The Great River Road, it snakes alongside the Mississippi River for more than 500 miles from Minnesota through Louisiana, popular with foodies, naturalists, and history enthusiasts alike

The Oregon Trail, it follows the historic path of 19th-century pioneers as they headed west, taking travelers 2,000 miles through mountains, valleys and prairies

The Olympic Peninsula Loop, at 330 miles long, it winds around Olympic National Park offering vistas of mountains, alpine lakes, forests and even a historic lighthouse

HISTORICAL PLACES TO VISIT IN THE U.S.

Okay, it's true: As far as history goes, the United States isn't that old. While Native Americans have lived here for thousands of years, the country itself is less than 300 years old. (Consider that Egypt has been a country for more than 5,000 years!) Still, it's accomplished a lot in its relatively short tenure, which provides plenty of historical attractions, museums, and memorials to add to your bucket list:

Watch a Revolutionary War, Civil War, or WWII reenactment

Lincoln Home National Historic Site, preserved by the National Park Service, it is where Abraham Lincoln lived before becoming the 16th president (Springfield, Ill)

Ford's Theatre, the historic site where Abraham Lincoln was assassinated in 1865, it's now a working theatre and museum (Washington, D.C.)

Ebenezer Baptist Church, Martin Luther King Jr.'s childhood church, it's considered central to the Civil Rights Movement (Atlanta)

Plymouth Rock, the Pilgrim Memorial State Park, it is the symbolic landing site of the Mayflower Pilgrims in 1620 (Plymouth, Mass.)

Plimoth Plantation, interactions between 17th century English settlers and local Wampanoag people come to life with a reconstructed Mayflower II docked at the waterfront as well as homes and actors representing both populations (Plymouth, Mass.)

Boston Harbor, visit the historic harbor famous for the Boston Tea Party (Boston)

Boston Tea Party Museum, located where and with a replica of the tea clipper where the event actually occurred, actors help tell the story of this iconic event (Boston)

41

The Alamo, site of the 1836 Battle of the Alamo, it's an iconic symbol of Texan independence (San Antonio, Texas)

The National Mall, here you'll find the nation's most famous monuments to presidents including Washington, Lincoln, Jefferson and more (Washington, D.C.)

Statue of Liberty, a gift from France in 1886, it symbolizes the American ideals of equality, democracy, and freedom (New York)

Mount Rushmore, the iconic faces of four U.S. presidents (Washington, Jefferson, Lincoln, and Roosevelt) are carved into the Black Hills (Keystone, S.D.)

Harriet Tubman Underground Railroad, commemorates and honors her life and legacy as a conductor on the Underground Railroad (Church Creek, Md.)

Nook Farm, Mark Twain's home from 1874 to 1891, this is where he wrote "The Adventures of Tom Sawyer" (Hartford, Conn.)

Edgar Allan Poe's grave (Baltimore, Md.)

Antietam National Battlefield, preserved Civil War battlefield and cemetery is the site of the bloodiest single-day battle in American history (Sharpsburg, Md.)

Gettysburg National Military Park, the historic Civil War battlefield was a turning point in the war and precipitated Lincoln's Gettysburg Address that honored the men who fought and died there (Gettysburg, Pa.)

Mount Vernon, George Washington's plantation home overlooking the Potomac River, now a preserved estate (Mount Vernon, Va.)

Monticello, Thomas Jefferson's neoclassical estate was designed by Jefferson and includes his burial place (Charlottesville, Va.)

The Legacy Museum, chronicles the history of racial inequality and injustice in America (Montgomery, Ala.)

Serpent Mound, an ancient effigy mound in the shape of a snake with a curled tail, it dates back over 1,000 years to ancient Native Americans (Peebles, Ohio)

Garnet Ghost Town, this was a gold mining town in the late 1800s, but today is a preserved ghost town you can tour (Drummond, Mont.)

Huff Indian Village State Historic Site, preserves ancient settlement from pre-contact Plains Indian culture, dating to about AD 1450 in pristine condition (Huff, N.D.)

Laura Ingalls Wilder Historic Homes, includes various restored homes of the beloved author that offers an immersive experience into pioneer life (De Smet, S.D.)

Pearl Harbor, infamous site of the 1941 attack by Japan, where more than 1,000 U.S. military members died (Honolulu, Hawaii)

Mesa Verde National Park, where you can view a preserved, ancient Pueblo cliff dwelling, built into the cliffs between 600-1300 AD (Colorado)

Ghost Ranch, Georgia O'Keeffe's summer home offered inspiration for the renowned artist (Abiquiu, N.M.)

National Museum of the U.S. Air Force, free for visitors, this is the world's largest military aviation museum with more than 360 aerospace vehicles, including the Memphis Belle and various presidential aircrafts you can walk through (Dayton, Ohio)

Smithsonian National Museum of American History, it features the original flag that inspired the Star-Spangled Banner as well as Abraham Lincoln's hat, Dorothy's ruby slippers and more (Washington, D.C.)

The National Museum of African American History and
Culture, it features more than 36,000 artifacts dedicated to
documenting the lives, experiences, and history of African
Americans (Washington, D.C.)

National Civil Rights Museum, it is in the hotel where
Martin Luther King Jr. was fatally shot and incorporates
historical facts as well as personal stories (Memphis, Tenn.)

The National Museum of the American Indian, its
exhibits spotlight the variety of Native American tribes and
their experiences, including the Trail of Tears and the Battle of
Little Bighorn (Washington, D.C.)

Autry Museum of the American West, it spotlights
specific histories such as pioneers, cowboys, the gold rush,
and Native Americans, as well as a garden dedicated to
Western plant life (Los Angeles)

The Museum of the American Revolution, takes visitors
on a chronological tour through the birth of the U.S. and
includes General George Washington's headquarters tent
(Philadelphia)

National WWI Museum and Memorial, houses the world's
most comprehensive collection of items from WWI and
features a glass suspension bridge over a symbolic Western
Front poppy field, that is a reminder of the 9 million who
perished during the war (Kansas City, Mo.)

National World War II Museum, you can explore the war
as it affected both the European and Pacific fronts, and
includes actual aircraft, tanks, and a submarine (New Orleans)

Henry Ford Museum, focuses on the history of
transportation with classic cars, retired presidential limousines,
an Oscar Mayer Wienermobile, and even the bus Rosa Parks
was arrested on (Detroit)

American Museum of Natural History, with more than 32 million specimens, exhibits include dinosaur fossils, meteorites, even human evolution (New York)

9/11 Memorial & Museum, located at the World Trade Center site, it's a tribute chronicling the events of that fateful day and honoring its victims (New York)

Ark Encounter, bringing the biblical story of Noah's Ark to life, it features a life-size replica of the ark and multiple immersive exhibits (Williamstown, Ky.)

Smithsonian National Air and Space Museum, showcases the evolution of flight and space exploration with artifacts including the Wright brothers' plane and the Apollo 11 command module (Washington, D.C.)

Cherokee Heritage Center, discover what life was like in a 1710 Cherokee village, featuring nearly 20 wattle and daub structures that include indoor and outdoor experiences (Tahlequah, Oklahoma)

Conner Prairie, travel through time with its 1816 Lenape Indian camp, 1836 prairie town, 1859 balloon voyage, 1863 Civil War and a variety of educational and adventurous opportunities (Fishers, Indiana)

Genesee Country Village & Museum, the third-largest living history museum in the country, 68 restored, historical buildings, heirloom gardens, actors and livestock bring the past to life from 1790 through 1900 (Mumford, N.Y.)

National Underground Railroad Freedom Center, shares the stories of freedom's heroes from the era of the Underground Railroad until now, with exhibits including a recovered slave pen from the 1800s, multiple films and other interactive features (Cincinnati)

45

Ponce de Leon's Fountain of Youth Archeological Park, commemorates the founding of St. Augustine, America's first colony, having been settled in 1565, decades before the pilgrims landed at Plymouth Rock; exhibits include a Native American Timucuan village, mission house, blacksmith exhibit and the original spring that caught de Leon's eye (St. Augustine, Fla.)

Colonial Williamsburg, originally founded in 1699, the town has been restored to what it would have been like during the 18th century, complete with historic reenactments (Williamsburg, Va.)

VISIT A UNIQUE MUSEUM

By nature, humans are curious. So, there's a pretty good chance that—pick any interest or oddity—there's a museum dedicated to that. Museums exist for almost anything imaginable, whether it's for collections or brands, food or animals, events or hobbies. Here are some of our favorites, but consider this merely a jumping off point: What kind of museum would you like to explore?

The Bone Museum, the largest collection of human bones on the East Coast, it focuses on the history of medical osteology (Brooklyn, N.Y.)

Redner's Rescued Cat Figurine Mewseum, a private home collection with 3,500+ cat figurines, which includes cookie jars, music boxes, even cat-inspired furniture (Menomonee Falls, Wis.)

Paranormal Roadtripper's Nightmare Gallery, a paranormal investigator showcases his collection which includes haunted objects, Bigfoot prints, and movie memorabilia (Somerset, Ky.)

The Insect Asylum, features thousands of preserved bugs and offers hands-on classes where you can learn how to taxidermy and pin butterflies (Chicago)

Santa Claus Museum, more than 3,000 pieces featuring Saint Nick fill this small museum, where he festoons everything from jump-rope handles to Coca-Cola bottles, as well as figurines from cultures around the world (Columbus, Texas)

Showgirl Magic Museum, dedicated to the history of showgirls with authentic costumes, photographs and memorabilia (San Francisco)

Portland Puppet Museum, this collection includes more than 2,000 puppets from more than 38 countries, and notable specimen such as an original Miss Piggy, a reproduction of Lamb Chop and Topo Gigio from *The Ed Sullivan Show* (Portland)

American Bookbinders Museum, discover the history of books, from its earliest form on clay tablets and scrolls through the modern era with cast iron machinery (San Francisco)

International Quilt Museum, home to the world's largest quilt collection, with quilts dating from the 1600s through today (Lincoln, Neb.)

Volo Auto Museum, founded in 1960 by a family-run dealership, it now spans 35 acres with iconic classics including the original Batmobile, a Scooby Doo Mystery Machine van, the DeLorean from *Back to the Future*, as well as multiple celebrity vehicles (Volo, Ill.)

The Museum at Fashion Institute of Technology, it has a permanent collection of more than 50,000 garments and accessories from the 18th century to now, earning it the moniker "the most fashionable museum in New York City" (New York)

Neon Museum, features 250 retro neon signs that originally decorated the Las Vegas Strip (Las Vegas)

International Spy Museum, the only public museum in the country dedicated to espionage, visitors are given cover identities as they gather intel and crack codes (Washington, D.C.)

Roswell UFO Museum, dedicated to the 1947 Roswell UFO crash that the military claims was merely a weather balloon, the collection features evidence and tracks the history of UFO events (Roswell, N.M.)

SPAM Museum, with free admission, you can learn all about the history of SPAM, see a recreation of Hormel's Provision Market and even discover how tall you are in cans of SPAM (Austin, Minn.)

Rock & Roll Hall of Fame, view memorabilia from the likes of Elvis Presley, the Beatles and more as the museum showcases the history of the genre (Cleveland, Ohio)

Museum of Pop Culture, known as MoPOP, this nonprofit museum is dedicated to showcasing the most iconic moments in pop culture (Seattle)

Mob Museum, located in the old federal building where one of the most famous mob trials occurred, learn about the history of organized crime and have fun with interactive exhibits like the Crime Lab and Weapon Simulators (Las Vegas)

The Grammy Museum, features interactive exhibits, actual instruments you can play, as well as memorabilia from famous artists (Los Angeles)

Country Music Hall of Fame & Museum, honoring country music legends, this museum houses more than 2.5 million artifacts (Nashville, Tenn.)

WHAT'S ON YOUR BUCKET LIST?

LEAVE A *Review*

DID WE HELP YOU THINK OF NEW PLACES TO GO OR THINGS TO TRY?
SHARE YOUR SHORT REVIEW HERE:

THEY REALLY HELP!

PART III

world Travel BUCKET LIST *ideas*

The world where we live is vast: Its circumference alone stretches nearly 25,000 miles at the equator. It includes nearly 200 different countries you could visit. Even more impressive, researchers estimate that there are at least 3,800 different distinct cultures present throughout the world, today. So, why not start exploring some of those? The lists in this next section will help you build a bucket list that does just that!

THINGS TO EXPERIENCE
AROUND THE WORLD

Here are some goals for your worldwide-travel bucket list, some of which are more open-ended and some of which are more ambitious. Which ones speak to you?

Create a map of all the places you've travelled around the world

Visit a certain number of countries (ie, 50, 100, etc.)

Visit every continent

Visit both the North and South Poles

Visit the equator

Visit the International Date Line

Visit all five oceans of the world (Atlantic, Pacific, Indian, Arctic and Southern Oceans)

Visit a country where you don't speak the language

Learn to say key phrases in a foreign language while traveling

Learn cultural customs in countries you visit

Visit a native or indigenous people in a different country

Visit the countries where you might have ancestral roots

Visit ancient ruins in another country

Visit the most famous seas of the world (such as the Caribbean, Mediterranean, Arabian, Red and Aegean Seas)

Visit the most famous rainforests of the world (such as the Amazon, Congo, Australasian, and Sundaland rainforests)

Visit the most famous deserts of the world (such as the Sahara, Gobi, Negev, and Namib Deserts)

- Visit a castle (the most total castles for a single country are in Germany, but the most castles found per square mile are in Wales)

- Visit a graveyard and pay your respects to the dead in another country

- Visit a museum in another country

- Try ethnic foods in another country

- Visit an outdoor marketplace in another country (such as the Grand Bazaar in Istanbul, Turkey; the Tsukiji Market in Tokyo; or the Queen Victoria Market in Melbourne, Australia)

VISIT THE SEVEN WONDERS OF THE MODERN WORLD

It was 200 BCE when the original list of the Seven Wonders of the World was created. However, since then, only one of those original wonders remains—the Pyramids of Giza. That's why, in 2000, a Swiss foundation took up the task to create a new list featuring the top Seven Wonders of the World that can still be seen today. Consider visiting one of these wonders on Seven Wonders Day, July 7!

Great Wall of China, it's the largest man-made project in the world, which took more than 2,000 years to construct (China)

Chichén Itzá, one of the largest ancient Mayan cities, it includes a large step pyramid temple (Mexico)

Petra, an ancient rock-cut city carved out of sandstone, earning it the moniker "Rose City" (Jordan)

Machu Picchu, an Inca citadel from the 15th century, located in the mountains above the Sacred Valley (Peru)

Christ the Redeemer, a giant statue of Jesus Christ towers 98 feet tall on the peak of Corcovado mountain (Rio de Janeiro, Brazil)

Colosseum, the largest amphitheater ever built, it could hold over 50,000 spectators in ancient Rome (Rome)

Taj Mahal, carved from white marble, it's a grand mausoleum for the Shah and his wife (Agra, India)

PLACES TO VISIT IN NORTH & SOUTH AMERICA

As the third- and fourth-largest continents in the world, North and South America are found in the Western Hemisphere and are home to a great swath of natural, geologic, cultural, and historical gems that are worth adding to your bucket list. While we listed all of our favorites for the United States in PART II, here are some of our favorites from elsewhere on these continents:

The Amazon Rain Forest, the world's largest rainforest, it spans nine countries and is home to diverse wildlife and indigenous cultures (Brazil, Bolivia, Peru, Ecuador, Colombia, Venezuela, Guyana, Suriname)

Easter Island, nearly 900 iconic moai statues (human figures with oversized heads) weighing 14 tons each were carved from volcanic rock during the 13th to 16th centuries (Easter Island, Chile)

The Galápagos Islands, spanning multiple islands, they are famous for their large number of endemic species studied by Charles Darwin (Ecuador)

Salar de Uyuni, the world's largest salt flat, it was previously a prehistoric lake that is now dry, creating stunning mirror effects in its white salt that is estimated to contain 10 billion tons of salt (Potosí, Bolivia)

Parque Natural Metropolitano, this tropical rain forest is the only one in the world located within a capital city (Panama City, Panama)

Bermuda Triangle, where more than 50 airplanes and ships are said to have mysteriously disappeared (Atlantic Ocean between Bermuda, Florida, and Puerto Rico)

Sulfur Springs, this is the world's only drive-in volcano, where you can drive into and witness bubbling sulfur springs, though the volcano itself is now dormant (Malgretoute, St. Lucia)

Molinere Underwater Sculpture Park, featuring 75 underwater sculptures, it was the first of its kind, accessible while scuba-diving and snorkeling (The Lime, Grenada)

Angel Falls, the world's tallest, uninterrupted waterfall, it's 19 times taller than Niagara Falls, stretching more than 3,200 feet from top to bottom (Canaima National Park, Venezuela)

Atacama Desert, West of the Andes Mountains, this stretch of desert is one of the world's driest places, with some areas having not received a drop of rain in 400 years (Chile)

PLACES TO VISIT IN EUROPE

Europe is the second smallest of Earth's continents. Yet, despite being small in size, it consists of 44 countries where more than 200 languages are spoken and more than 400 World Heritage Sites are located. Needless to say, it is abounding with a variety of cultural, architectural, and natural delights worthy for any bucket list. Here are some of our favorites:

London Bridge, spanning the River Thames, the original bridge was built in 1894 and the current version was built in 1973 (London)

Big Ben, a part of the Palace of Westminster, this iconic clock tower was completed in 1859 and still chimes every hour (London)

Leaning Tower, the freestanding bell tower completed in 1372 for the Pisa Cathedral, it is known for its 4-degree lean (Pisa, Italy)

Eiffel Tower, built for the 1889 World's Fair, it stands 1,063 feet and you can travel up 906 feet to view Paris from above (Paris)

The Acropolis, this ancient citadel overlooks the city of Athens and contains the remains of the Parthenon (Athens, Greece)

Santorini, situated on cliffs overlooking the Aegean Sea, it is a popular tourist destination (Santorini, Greece)

Anne Frank House, where she hid during WWII and wrote her diary, it is now a museum (Amsterdam)

Dyrehavsbakken, the world's oldest amusement park founded in 1583, it is free to enter, sits in the middle of the woods and includes 32 rides (Copenhagen, Denmark)

Foteviken Viking Museum, an open-air museum of a recreated Viking village from the early Middle Ages, it features 23 buildings and a reconstructed Viking ship (Höllviken, Sweden)

Neuschwanstein Castle, it was built in the 19th century in the foothills of the Alps and served as inspiration for Disney's Cinderella Castle (Schwangau, Germany)

Crystal Ice Cave, in Vatnajökull National Park, it's a cave-like structure inside Vatnajökull, the largest glacier in Europe (Skaftafell, Iceland)

Þingvellir National Park, where you can stand with one foot in America and one foot in Europe at the Mid-Atlantic Rift; also known for gorges, waterfalls, and even glacier-fed ravines for snorkeling (Selfoss, Iceland)

The Eden Project, tour giant, greenhouse-like biomes that house thousands of plant species; one biome is home to the world's largest indoor rainforest (Cornwall, England)

Keukenhof, features more than 7 million tulips, daffodils, and hyacinths each spring (Lisse, Netherlands)

ICEHOTEL, this hotel is carved out of ice each winter with rooms furnished with décor and beds made from ice for a real one-of-a-kind experience (Rukajarvi, Sweden)

Hill of Crosses, more than 100,000 crosses cover this hill; the tradition started in 1831 and served as a sign of resistance while the country was under Soviet rule (Jurgaičiai, Lithuania)

Old Orhei, a monastery complex carved into limestone cliffs along the Răut River during the 13th century (Trebujeni, Moldova)

Newborn monument, a typographic sculpture is repainted every year on Feb. 17 to memorialize the country's independence from Serbia (Prishtina, Kosovo)

Tara River Canyon, the continent's deepest river canyon (and only second in the world to the Grand Canyon), it features more than 100 caves, some the size of a house (Montenegro)

Perućica, one of the last remaining primeval forests in Europe, it dates back 20,000 years with some trees over 300 years old (Bosnia and Herzegovina)

Bigar Cascade Falls, hidden inside the Anina Mountains, it is considered by many to be the world's most unusual waterfall with its odd shape (Cheile Nerei-Beusnita National Park, Romania)

Bran Castle, the inspiration for Bram Stoker's story about Count Dracula, construction for it began in 1377 by King Louis I of Hungary to protect the country from the Ottoman Empire (Bran, Romania)

Wieliczka salt mines, begun in the 13th century, these salt mines have been exquisitely carved with chandeliers, chapels and even a rendering of the Last Supper (Wieliczka, Poland)

Prague Castle, the world's largest ancient castle, it dates to the 9th century and stretches longer than 5 soccer fields (Prague, Czechia)

Palace of Versailles, was the opulent home of King Louis XIV as well as the location of the Treaty of Versailles that ended WWI (Paris)

Swiss Alps, Matterhorn is one of this this mountain range's highest and most dangerous peaks; it also offers hiking, skiing and more (various countries including Switzerland)

Venice, made up of 118 islands connected by 150 canals, the city is famous for the gondolas that transport you through the city (Venice, Italy)

Aphrodite's Rock, this is where legend says the Greek goddess was born in the Mediterranean Sea (Paphos, Cyprus)

The Alhambra, it was the palace and fortress of Moorish monarchs, built in the 13th century featuring exceptional Islamic architecture (Granada, Spain)

Loch Ness, a large freshwater lake in the Scottish Highlands, famous for its supposed water monster, Nessie (Loch Ness, Scotland)

Mount Vesuvius, the volcano that erupted in 79 AD and destroyed Pompeii, you can hike to the crater rim that overlooks the Bay of Naples and see the Pompeii ruins (Campania, Italy)

Notre Dame Cathedral, built on an island in the Seine River during the 12th and 14th centuries, the iconic church survived a devastating fire in 2019 (Paris)

PLACES TO VISIT IN ASIA

Asia is the world's largest continent, taking up about 30 percent of the Earth's total land area. Its large expanse is home to 4.6 billion people in 48 countries including Russia, China, India, and the Middle East. Here are just some of the gems you'll find throughout different parts of Asia:

The Dead Sea, it is earth's lowest point, known for its high salt concentration that prohibits animal life as well as allows for effortless floating (Jordan/Israel)

Petronas Towers, twin skyscrapers connected with a sky bridge; they were the tallest buildings in the world until 2004 (Kuala Lumpur, Malaysia)

Troy, the archeological remains of the ancient city, made famous by the Greek myth about the Trojan War (Hisarlik, Turkey)

Shibam Hadramawt, known as "Manhattan of the Desert," it features 500, mudbrick-made high-rise homes that are the tallest mud structures in the world, having been built in the 16th century (Shibam Hadramawt, Yemen)

Pearl Qatar, considered an engineering feat, it is an artificial island that cost $15 billion to build on a site once famous for pearl diving (Doha, Qatar)

Kuwait Towers, the country's most famous landmark, these towers were built in 1979 with a blue mosaic design that's a nod to historic mosques (Kuwait City, Kuwait)

Great Ziggurat of Ur, this 4,000-year-old step pyramid was originally built by the Sumerians out of mud bricks as a shrine to their ancient gods (Nasiriyah, Iraq)

Cappadocia, features unique rock formations called "fairy chimneys" that are the result of volcanic erosion, it is a famous destination for scenic hot-air balloon rides (Turkey)

Adam's Peak, a mountain that is considered sacred to multiple religions, its rock formation at its top is considered to be the footprint of Buddha (Buddhism), Shiva (Hinduism) or Adam (Christianity and Islam) (Sabaragamuwa Province, Sri Lanka)

Sigiriya, an ancient, fortified garden city, this palace was built atop a towering rock in the 4th century; ornate frescos decorate the palace, which is considered one of the most elaborate urban planning sites of the time (Central Province, Sri Lanka)

Dubai Mall, it is the largest mall in the world, complete with the world's largest indoor aquarium, a theme park, and an Olympic-sized ice-skating rink, as well as an illusion waterfall and the world's biggest candy store (Dubai, UAE)

The Euphrates River, one of the two great rivers of Mesopotamia, it was of historical importance to ancient civilizations (Iraq, Syria)

The Palace Museum, housed in the Forbidden City, this imperial palace features an extensive Chinese art collection (Beijing)

The Kremlin, a historic fortress, it includes five palaces and four cathedrals as the political center of the Russian government (Moscow)

Saint Basil's Cathedral, an Orthodox church that now operates as a museum, its colorful onion-bulb domes and spires are one of the country's most iconic cultural symbols (Moscow)

Maldives, surrounded by picturesque coral reefs, these tropical islands make up the lowest-lying nation on earth, and is set to sink below sea level in the coming decades due to rising sea levels (Maldives)

Ijen volcano, sulfur vents cause it to burn in bright, neon colors: vibrant blue flames; yellow geysers; and a turquoise lake that is the world's largest acidic lake (Java, Indonesia)

Rainbow Mountains, these striking rock formations are naturally striped in blues, yellows, oranges, and reds due to mineral deposits that have mixed with sandstone over millions of years (Zhangye National Geopark, China)

Mount Fuji, this active volcano is a popular summit for hikers as well as religious pilgrims, consider it a sacred symbol (Mount Fuji, Japan)

PLACES TO VISIT IN AFRICA

It's believed that humanity's origins began in Africa, so why not return to your roots by adding some of the following hotspots to your bucket list? From deserts to beaches to snow-capped mountains, Africa has something for everyone!

The Nile River, Africa's longest river, it flows south to north and empties into the Mediterranean Sea, having been crucial to ancient Egypt (from Tanzania through Egypt)

Sahara Desert, the world's largest hot desert, it is about the size of China and home to Bedouin nomads who travel with camels (various, including Algeria)

Al-Sudd, one of the world's largest swamps, it is the size of England, with villages having been erected atop the water (South Sudan)

Valley of the Kings, about 300 miles from the Giza Pyramids, it was part of the ancient city of Themes and was the burial spot for 62 known pharaohs, including Ramses X (Luxor, Egypt)

The Serengeti, a vast savanna that hosts the Great Migration of wildebeest, zebras, and other wildlife (Tanzania)

Lake Turkana, the world's largest permanent desert lake, stretching 150 miles from north to south, it's known for its turquoise water where you can spot flamingos in the wild (Kenya)

Nairobi National Park, the world's only reserve where you'll find large, wild animals—think lions, leopards, and rhinos—while in an urban city (Nairobi, Kenya)

Great Mosque, it is the largest mud structure in the world, made entirely out of sunbaked mud bricks (Djenné, Mali)

Basilica of Our Lady Peace, the largest church in the world, it is inspired by Vatican City's St. Peter Basilica (Yamoussoukro, Ivory Coast)

The Congo, the deepest river in the world, it is also home to the world's second largest rainforest, where you'll find forest elephants, chimpanzees, bonobos, gorillas and more (various, including the Democratic Republic of Congo)

Laas Geel cave paintings, they are the oldest cave paintings in Africa, dating back more than 10,000 years to Neolithic times (Somaliland, Somalia)

Mount Kilimanjaro, this dormant volcano is the tallest mountain in Africa (though not part of a mountain chain) and one of the few places where you'll find snow in Africa! (Kilimanjaro National Park, Tanzania)

Hoba meteorite, the largest meteorite ever found on earth, it's estimated to weigh more than 60 tons and be over 80,000 years old (Hoba West, Namibia)

Great Zimbabwe ruins, a medieval city believed to have been built and actively inhabited from the 11th through 15th centuries, large stone structures are still visible, including a statue called the Zimbabwe Bird (Masvingo, Zimbabwe)

Cradle of Humankind, the site contains the largest concentration of human ancestral remains in the world, as well as more than 200 caves, which you can tour (Johannesburg, South Africa)

Table Mountain, one of the country's most iconic landmarks, it is also one of the oldest mountains in the world, often covered in thick clouds (Cape Town, South Africa)

PLACES TO VISIT IN AUSTRALIA & OCEANIA

Despite what you may have learned in grade school, technically, Australia is a part of Oceania, which is the smallest continent on the planet and includes other surrounding islands in the Pacific Ocean. In total, it consists of 14 countries and, as this list shows, quite a few worthwhile options to add to your bucket list:

Sydney Opera House, opened in 1973, it is home to various performing arts and is renowned for its distinctive architecture (Sydney, Australia)

The Pinnacles Desert, it contains thousands of weathered limestone pillars that tower over the landscape where Western grey kangaroos still graze (Nambung National Park, Australia)

Great Ocean Road, considered one of the most scenic roads in the world, it takes you past limestone stacks known as Twelve Apostles, which were naturally formed by erosion (Victoria, Australia)

Outback, known as one of the most desolate places on earth, it is made up of 10 deserts, a sub-tropical savanna and the world's largest temperate woodland, and covers most of the country (various, Australia)

Daintree Rainforest, at 180 million years old, it is the oldest rainforest on Earth, and home to the elusive Cassowary bird, Mossman Gorge and a white-sand beach (Queensland, Australia)

Kakadu National Park, a diverse wilderness with wetlands and waterfalls, it is also where you can spot Aboriginal rock art (Northern Territory, Australia)

Bora Bora, sitting atop an extinct volcano, it is renowned for its lagoons, black pearls, and heart-shaped coral reef (French Polynesia)

Tongariro National Park, home to the iconic Tongariro Alpine Crossing, it is also the country's oldest national park with volcanic landscapes, active craters, and emerald lakes (North Island, New Zealand)

Waitomo Glowworm Caves, renowned for their mesmerizing bioluminescent glowworm displays that illuminate dark caverns like a starlit sky (Waitomo, New Zealand)

Fiordland National Park, known for glacier-carved fiords, waterfalls, snow-capped peaks, and an ancient rainforest that has remained unchanged for a thousand years (South Island, New Zealand)

The International Date Line, passes through Fiji, dividing the world into its Eastern and Western hemispheres—meaning that it's different days on either side of the imaginary line (Taveuni, Fiji)

To-Sua Ocean Trench, literally meaning, "giant swimming hole," you can jump off a platform into the teal-blue waters, 98 feet below (Upolu, Samoa)

FESTIVALS FROM AROUND THE WORLD TO ATTEND

Who doesn't love a party? That's why you'll find festivals and parades everywhere you go. But the ones featured on this list are among the most festive ones around—and for good reason. Big, bold and with plenty of personality, each of these are celebrations worth checking out:

Rio Carnival, a colorful parade through the streets with samba music and elaborate costumes (Rio de Janeiro)

Oktoberfest, celebrating traditional Bavarian culture, music, food, and beer (Munich)

Holi, the festival of colors marking the arrival of spring (throughout India)

Diwali, the Festival of Lights, is celebrated with fireworks and other illuminated decorations (Mumbai, India)

Songkran, celebrating the Thai New Year, it's known for water games symbolizing the cleansing and renewal of the spirit (Bangkok)

Running of the Bulls, where participants run in the streets alongside six to ten bulls as a part of the San Fermín festival held in July (Pamplona, Spain)

Cherry Blossom Festival, celebrates the tree and its pink blooms each spring, having been celebrated since the 8th century (throughout Japan)

Day of the Dead, known as Día de los Muertos, this holiday honors deceased loved ones through colorful altars, parades, and traditional rituals (Mexico City)

St. Patrick's Day, a national holiday, its annual parade features floats, marching bands and various performances and cultural celebrations (Dublin)

Elephant Festival, celebrates highly decorated elephants (as well as camels, horses, and folk dancers) with elephants competing in polo, tug of war and more (Jaipur, India)

Harbin International Ice and Snow Sculpture Festival, the world's largest festival of its kind, where ice sculptures are erected throughout the city (Harbin, China)

Sziget Music Festival, often voted Europe's best music festival, it features more than one thousand performances across multiple genres (Budapest, Hungary)

The Flower Carpet, more than 1,500 begonias, dahlias, grass, and bark are assembled to create a giant "carpet" of flowers that stretches more than 18,000 square feet (Brussels)

La Tomatina, the world's largest food fight: 110 tons of overripe tomatoes are thrown each year, memorializing a 1945 street brawl that erupted near a vegetable street stand (Buñol, Spain)

FIESA Sand and Sculpture Festival, 44 tons of sand are transformed over 90 days into the world's most incredible sand structures (Pêra, Portugal)

Macy's Thanksgiving Day Parade, it features giant balloons that float through the streets of New York on Thanksgiving morning (New York)

Mardi Gras, the highlight is a parade featuring elaborate floats where beaded necklaces are thrown to the crowd (New Orleans)

Chinese New Year Parade, the largest one in the world, it features floats, performances and a giant Golden Dragon that takes 100 people to carry (San Francisco)

Festival of Lights, internationally renowned artists transform the city into one giant art exhibit with impressive light shows and illuminated displays on building exteriors (Sharjah, United Arab Emirates)

FAMOUS POP-CULTURE DESTINATIONS AROUND THE WORLD

Fame can make people do crazy things. Fortunately, it can also immortalize certain places, thanks to the role they played in giving birth to iconic scenes and even the celebrity, him- or herself. Check out this list of places that you can visit that pay homage to a variety of pop-culture icons, and see if any of them make your bucket list:

The Goonies movie was filmed at a house still located in Astoria, Ore.

Johnny Cash, tour his restored, boyhood home in Dyess, Ark.

Home Alone movie, filmed at a house located in Winnetka, Ill.

Graceland, Elvis Presley's home in Memphis, Tenn. is the second most-visited house in the country, after the White House

The Brady Bunch original television show was filmed in a house in North Hollywood, Calif.

Downtown Abbey, the television show was filmed at the Highclere Castle in Hampshire, England

Henry Ford's home, Fair Lane, is open to the public to explore the 1,300-acre grounds in Dearborn, Mich.

Stranger Things, television show was filmed at a house in Fayetteville, Ga.

John Lennon and Paul McCartney's childhood homes are both open for tours in Liverpool, England

Schitt's Creek, the television show's Rosebud Motel can be found in Ontario

Dollywood, founded by Dolly Parton in Pigeon Forge, Tenn., is an amusement park which includes a replica of her childhood home (a two-room log cabin)

Breaking Bad, the television show was filmed at a house in Albuquerque, N.M.

Full House, the television show featured the exterior of a house in San Francisco

Louis Armstrong's former home is now a museum in Queens, New York, dedicated to the artist's jazz career

The Fresh Prince of Bel Air, the television show featured a house not in Bel Air, but Brentwood, Calif.

Ernest Hemingway's Spanish Colonial-style home, where he lived for ten years and wrote 70 percent of his works, is now a museum in Key West, Fla., complete with the progeny of his 6-toed cats still in residence

Friends, the television show's apartment building is in New York's Greenwich Village

Ferris Bueller's Day Off, the movie was filmed at a house in Highland Park, Ill.

The Wonder Years, the television show was filmed at a house located in Burbank, Calif.

Judy Garland's childhood home is now a museum, where you can view a pair of her ruby red slippers from The Wizard of Oz in Grand Rapids, Minn.

Pirates of the Caribbean, filmed in and around the Caribbean islands of St. Vincent and the Grenadines

Game of Thrones, filmed in an avenue of beech trees along Bregagh Road in Ballymoney, Northern Ireland

Star Wars movies shot in Tunisian deserts, including Mos Espa, Ong Jemel and Sidi Bouhlel

Disneyland, Disney's original theme park in Anaheim, Cali., it opened in 1955 and is famous for rides including Space Mountain, Jungle Cruise and more

The Lord of the Rings and **The Hobbit** trilogies' Middle-earth Hobbiton set was built and can be toured in Matamata, New Zealand

VISIT ONE OF THE WORLD'S MOST HAUNTED PLACES

Do you binge watch scary movies? Or live for all-things Halloween? Why not take that to the next level by adding one of these sites—reputed to be among the most haunted in the world—to your bucket list?!

Villisca Ax Murder House, the site of a brutal 1912 murder of eight people that remains unsolved (Villisca, Iowa)

Poinsett Bridge, the oldest bridge in the state, legends say it's haunted by the workers and slaves who helped build it (Landrum, S.C.)

Lizzie Borden House, now a museum and bed and breakfast, it's the home of the 1892 unsolved murder of Lizzie Borden's father and stepmother (Fall River, Mass.)

Alcatraz Island, once a military prison, Native Americans also believed it to be cursed by evil spirits (San Francisco)

Eastern State Penitentiary, this crumbling castle, where Al Capone was a former inmate, it has appeared on numerous ghost-hunting shows, which claim to have captured unexplainable evidence of hauntings (Philadelphia)

Fairmont Banff Springs, more than a century old, this hotel is supposedly haunted by former guests and workers, including a bellhop and veiled bride (Banff, Canada)

Island of the Dolls, after finding a drowned a girl in its waters, a man attempted to appease her spirit by hanging dolls around the island; now, tourists add to the island's collection (Laguna de Tequila, Mexico)

La Recoleta Cemetery, this graveyard is supposedly haunted by multiple ghosts including a gravedigger, "The Lady in White," and a woman buried alive (Buenos Aires, Argentina)

Tower of London, a historic castle built on the River Thames, it is said to be haunted by more than a dozen ghosts, including Anne Boleyn, Lady Jane Grey, Guy Fawkes and even a grizzly bear (London)

Edinburgh Castle, one of its most famous ghosts is the piper, who supposedly was sent to explore the tunnels beneath the castle, never to be seen again (Edinburgh, Scotland)

Hoia-Baciu Forest, it earned its name after a shepherd and his flock of 200 sheep supposedly disappeared into the forest; is the site of a UFO sighting; and has been featured on multiple paranormal television shows (Transylvania, Romania)

Paris Catacombs, an underground labyrinth, it houses the most graves in the world—six million! —giving rise to many tales of hauntings (Paris)

Château de Brissac, the site of a double murder, it is now supposedly haunted by the Green Lady (Brissac Loire Aubance, France)

Zvikov Castle, built in the 13th century, its towers are believed to have been haunted by a demonic imp for hundreds of years (Zvíkovské Podhradí, Czech Republic)

Borgvattnet Vicarage, built in 1876, it is said to be the country's most haunted spot; it is now a bed-and-breakfast where you can stay overnight (Borgvattnet, Sweden)

Castle of Good Hope, a fortress with a dungeon in the basement, it is said to be haunted by former prisoners, soldiers and even a black dog (Cape Town, South Africa)

Monte Cristo Homestead, reported to be haunted by the ghosts of more than 10 former inhabitants and servants of the home (Junee, Australia)

Aradale Mental Hospital, the institution ran for 126 years, during which time more than 13,000 patients and staff died within its walls, who are reported to still haunt and terrorize it to this day (Victoria, Australia)

Lawang Sewu, once home to the Dutch East Indies Railway Company, it became a prison during WWII, resulting in many of its reported ghosts who were decapitated during their stay (Semarang, Indonesia)

BRING YOUR BUCKET LIST TO LIFE WITH THE COMPANION PLANNING JOURNAL!

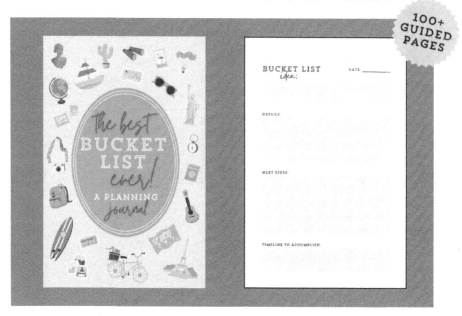

TURN YOUR DREAMS INTO REALITY!

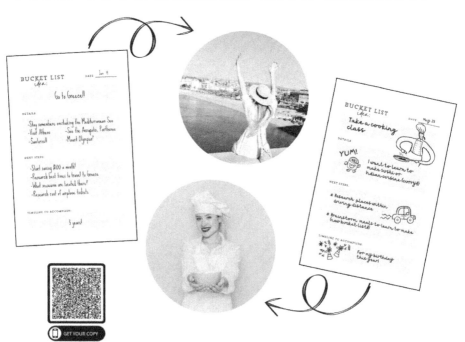

PART IV

other BUCKET LIST ideas

As much as we love traveling, there are lots of other things that can (and should!) be considered for your bucket list. Things that aren't bound by lines of latitude and longitude or that you could even check off in your own hometown. From fine dining to religious experiences, athletics events to entertainment, browse these lists for interests that appeal to you for your bucket list!

THINGS TO DO —THAT WON'T BREAK THE BANK!

Bucket lists do not have to cost a lot money. We'll say it again: They can be affordable! Cheap! Free, even! Here is a list of options that won't break the bank but will still make for unforgettable memories on your bucket list.

- Get your picture taken in a photobooth
- Fly a kite
- Give up your smartphone for a day
- Go on a social-media fast
- Sleep under the stars
- Plan a picnic in the park
- Be a tourist in your own town
- Go camping in your backyard
- Host a game night
- Create a time capsule
- Volunteer (see list, p. 97)
- Binge watch a favorite movie or television show
- Shop at an outdoor market
- Go to a flea market or outdoor garage sale
- Host a garage sale
- Go shopping at an antique or thrift store
- Play frisbee
- Paint and hide kindness rocks
- Go metal-detecting
- Go geocaching

EXPLORE YOUR OWN PERSONAL HISTORY

In ancient Greece, it is inscribed on the Temple of Apollo: "Know thyself." That maxim rings as true today as it did centuries ago, which is why it's worth incorporating activities into your bucket list that help you do just that:

- Take a personality test
- Find out what your love language is
- Take a test to determine your strengths and weaknesses
- Learn your enneagram number
- Have your handwriting analyzed
- Learn more about your astrological sign
- Explore therapy
- Try self-hypnosis
- Keep a dream journal
- Complete an ancestry DNA test
- Learn more about the places where your family is from
- Research the meaning of your first name
- Research the meaning of your last name
- See if you have a family crest
- (If not, design a family crest of your own!)
- Take time to get to know a member of your family better
- Research your family genealogy
- Look through library, newspaper, county and state records for any of your ancestors
- Document your family tree
- Create your own personal motto
- Attend or plan a family reunion

STYLE & SELF-CARE
THINGS TO INDULGE IN

We all talk about how important self-care is—which is exactly why you should consider incorporating it into your bucket list! That's what this list is all about—ideas to pamper your body and soul:

- Start seeing a counselor
- Start a journal
- Start a daily gratitude list
- Practice meditation
- Practice deep-breathing
- Take a bubble bath
- Create your personal list of affirmations
- Get a tattoo
- Get a henna tattoo
- Design your own T-shirt
- Dye your hair
- Try a new haircut
- Get your makeup professionally done
- Skip the makeup
- Do a DIY photoshoot
- Have a professional photoshoot
- Have a spa day
- Buy yourself flowers
- Host a clothing-swap party
- Attend a fashion show
- Appear in a fashion show
- Wear a wig
- Build a capsule wardrobe
- Test out a new make-up trend
- Try out a new fashion trend
- Get a manicure
- Get a pedicure
- Try a mud mask
- Get a massage
- Try a hot stone massage
- Get a facial
- Get a body mask
- Try out a sauna
- Try aromatherapy
- Try float therapy/sensory deprivation tank

ARTISTIC & CREATIVE ENDEAVORS TO TRY

Pablo Picasso once said, "Every child is an artist. The problem is how to remain an artist once he grows up." Well, this list should help with that. Full of ideas spanning several disciplines, it will help get your creative juices flowing. Who knows what masterpiece awaits you?!

- Learn a language
- Write a book
- Publish that book
- Audition for a play
- Learn to play an instrument
- Start a band
- Take a pottery class
- Learn how to blow glass
- Pick flowers and make a bouquet
- Learn to hand letter
- Sew something
- Enter your art in a competition
- Join or start your own book club
- Read 100 books in a year
- Read a classic book
- Write a song
- Post that song on YouTube
- Memorize a poem
- Attend an art opening
- Go to an art museum (see list, p. 82)
- Buy a large canvas paint your own piece of modern art

TOP ART MUSEUMS
AROUND THE WORLD TO VISIT

Did you know that simply viewing art in a museum has been shown to decrease stress? You probably don't have to be a scientist to realize that, but making great art a priority on your bucket list seems like a given. As a result, here are some of the best art museums around the world. (Can you feel your body relaxing already?!)

Tate Modern, opened by Queen Elizabeth II in 2000, it is one of the newest museums but still draws millions of visitors each year to its collection, focusing on modern art from the likes of Andy Warhol, Dali, and Picasso (London)

Louvre, the world's largest and most popular art museum, it features Da Vinci's *Mona Lisa* (Paris)

Van Gogh Museum, dedicated solely to the artist who hails from the Netherlands, it has 1,300 of his works, including *Sunflowers* (Amsterdam)

The Rijksmuseum, contains more than 1 million pieces of art from 1200 AD to the modern day, including an original Rembrandt (Amsterdam)

The State Hermitage Museum, only the Louvre is larger than this museum, which has more than 3,000 pieces from artists including Picasso, Da Vinci and Rembrandt (St. Petersburg, Russia)

Musée d'Orsay, houses the world's largest collection of impressionist and post-impressionist masterpieces in the world (Paris)

The Vatican Museums, the world's oldest art museum, having opened in 1506, it features works such as the Sistine Chapel and the Raphael Rooms (Vatican City)

National Gallery, its collection of more than 2,300 pieces includes ones by Michelangelo, Da Vinci and Monet (London)

Metropolitan Museum of Art, also known as the Met, it has more than 2 million artefacts and only the Louvre boasts more visitors (New York)

Museum of Modern Art, also known as MoMA, it holds the world's largest collection of contemporary art with more than 150,000 pieces (New York)

National Art Center, established in 2007, it's an "empty museum," only hosting travelling exhibits rather than its own permanent exhibits (Tokyo)

Shanghai Museum, it boasts more than 120,000 pieces, with a large collection of Chinese art including one of three mirrors from the Han Dynasty (Shanghai)

Getty Museum, features art from ancient civilizations through the present, it includes work by Monet, Van Gogh, Rembrandt, and Degas (Los Angeles)

ENTERTAINMENT & EVENTS TO EXPERIENCE

There's a reason people packed the Colosseum in ancient Rome and Shakespeare's plays have been captivating audiences for hundreds of years: Entertainment has long been the heartbeat of humanity, providing much-needed breaks from everyday life. That need is as vital today as it was thousands of years ago, so consider adding one of these awe-inspiring attractions and amusements to your bucket list:

- See a play
- Attend a Broadway show
- Attend a rodeo
- Meet someone famous
- Sing karaoke
- Go to a drive-in movie
- Apply to be on a reality show
- Attend a murder mystery show
- Complete an escape room
- Go to a music festival
- See a game show live
- Learn a dance (hula, belly, line dancing, or even the Macarena!)
- Go to a book signing
- Learn a magic trick
- Ride a mechanical bull
- See a ballet
- Visit an amusement park
- See your favorite band perform live
- Go to a comedy show

- [ ] Take an improv class
- [ ] March in a parade
- [ ] Attend a masquerade ball
- [ ] Walk on a red carpet
- [ ] Attend a film premiere
- [ ] See a fashion show
- [ ] Visit a museum
- [ ] Take a boat tour
- [ ] Visit a botanical garden
- [ ] Visit a state or national monument
- [ ] Visit an arboretum
- [ ] Visit a science center
- [ ] See a demolition derby
- [ ] Check out a monster truck rally
- [ ] Watch a tractor pull competition
- [ ] Go to a hot rod car show
- [ ] Attend an air show
- [ ] Go to the circus
- [ ] Take a circus class (trapeze, tightrope, clown, magic, etc.)
- [ ] Join a drum circle
- [ ] Attend a jousting tournament
- [ ] Visit a Renaissance faire or festival
- [ ] Go to a state or county fair
- [ ] Attend comic-con
- [ ] Watch a food-eating competition
- [ ] Participate in a food-eating competition

SPORTS & ATHLETICS GOALS WORTH ACHIEVING

Sporting events have been around for thousands of years. Even cave paintings depict athletes competing! Not only do they keep us fit, they also have been shown to improve our mental health and boost confidence. So why not add one of these exercise- or sports-related activities or destinations to your bucket list adventures?

- Participate in a 5K/marathon
- Dress up in a funny costume for a 5K/marathon
- Participate in a "color run"
- Go bowling
- Go glow-in-the-dark bowling
- Climb an indoor rock wall
- Watch a BMX bike competition
- See motocross
- Play pickleball
- Go roller skating
- Drive a golf cart
- Participate in a mud run
- Go canoeing
- Go kayaking
- Play mini golf
- Go to the driving range
- Go ice-skating
- See a roller derby
- Try a cold plunge

- Attend the Summer Olympic Games (varies)

- Attend the Winter Olympic Games (varies)

- Attend the World Series, the annual Major League Baseball championship (varies)

- Attend the Super Bowl, the annual National Football League championship (varies)

- Attend the World Cup, the international soccer competition (varies)

- Attend the Kentucky Derby, the thoroughbred horse race, known as "the greatest two minutes in sports" (Louisville, Ky.)

- Attend the Masters Tournament for golf (Augusta, Ga.)

- Attend the Daytona 500 stock car race (Daytona, Fla.)

- Attend the Indianapolis 500 Indy car race (Indianapolis)

- Attend the Stanley Cup, the annual National Hockey League championship (varies)

- Attend the US Open Tennis Championship (Queens, N.Y)

- Attend the Wimbledon, the world's oldest tennis tournament (London)

- Attend the Tour de France annual bicycle race (France)

- Attend the Italian Grand Prix Formula 1 car race (Monza, Italy)

- Attend the NBA Finals, the annual championship series of the National Basketball Association (varies)

- Attend a NCAA Final Four basketball game (varies)

- Attend the Iditarod dog sled racing (Anchorage to Nome, Alaska)

- Attend the Highland Games, celebrating Scottish and Celtic culture with traditional games like the caber toss, tug o' war and the hammer throw (Scotland)

Attend the Rose Bowl, an annual American college football bowl game traditionally played on Jan. 1 (Pasadena, Calif.)

Visit Wrigley Field, home of the Chicago Cubs baseball team (Chicago)

Visit Yankee Stadium, home to the New York Yankees baseball team (New York)

Visit Fenway Park, home to the Boston Red Sox baseball team (Boston)

Visit Madison Square Garden, home to the New York Knicks basketball team (New York)

Visit the Notre Dame Stadium, home to the Fighting Irish football team for University of Notre Dame (Notre Dame, Ind.)

Visit Lambeau Field, home of the Green Bay Packers football team (Green Bay, Wis.)

FOOD & CULINARY IDEAS
TO SAVOR

Julia Child once said, "People who love to eat are always the best people." So be your best! This list is chockfull of food- and cooking-related bucket-list ideas that will allow you to eat, drink and be merry:

- Look up a recipe for your favorite meal from a restaurant and make it
- Make your own _____ from scratch (bread, pasta, cheese, pickles, kimchi, etc.)
- Bake and sculpt a cake into a shape (football, heart, mermaid, rainbow, etc.)
- Try a food from a different culture (then, learn to make it yourself!)
- Try a local delicacy on your travels
- Eat with chop sticks
- Recreate your favorite foods from childhood
- Make a family recipe
- Pick your own fruit (apple, strawberry, blueberry, etc.)
- Visit a farmer's market
- Attend a traditional tea service (English, Chinese, etc.)
- Try the weirdest ice-cream flavor in the shop
- Try a Carolina Reaper pepper
- Try deep-fried _____ (Oreos, Twinkies, pickles, bacon, etc.)
- Visit a local ethnic supermarket and try a new food or drink
- Tour a factory for your favorite food (see list, p. 90)
- Find a festival for your favorite food (see list, p. 92)
- Visit the original restaurant of your favorite chain restaurant (see list, p. 90)

FAVORITE FOOD DESTINATIONS AROUND THE U.S.

Do you have a favorite snack or brand of sweet that you still gobble up, whenever you see it? Or a favorite restaurant you'll drive out of your way for? We all do, which is why we compiled this list dedicated to some of our most beloved brands and treats:

Jelly Belly Visitor Center, the quarter-mile tour features interactive exhibits, games, an art gallery, and the most unusual jelly-bean flavors imaginable (Fairfield, Calif.)

PEZ Visitor's Center, features the largest collection of PEZ memorabilia in the world, games, and behind-the-scenes peeks into the production area (Orange, Conn.)

Cape Cod Factory Tour, see how the kettle-cooked potato chips are made, and even receive a complimentary bag of chips! (Cape Cod, Mass.)

Starbucks Reserve, offers private tours and exclusive beverage tastings (Seattle, Chicago, New York)

Tillamook Creamery, learn about the company's history over the past one hundred years and even participate in an ice-cream tasting (Tillamook, Ore.)

HERSHEY'S Chocolate World, see how the chocolate is made, plus enjoy samples; a Hersheypark theme park is also here (Hershey, Penn.)

Ben & Jerry's original factory tour takes you behind the scenes of how the brand's ice cream is made with additional VIP experiences available (Waterbury, Vt.)

World of Coca-Cola, a 20-acre complex showcasing the history of Coca-Cola with exhibits about its secret recipe and a tasting room with 60 flavors from around the world (Atlanta)

McDonald's, the original restaurant opened in 1940 and is now a museum where you can view memorabilia and find out the history chronicling the restaurant's rise (San Bernardino, Calif.)

Chipotle Mexican Grill, the original restaurant launched in 1993 near the University of Denver Campus and is still in operation for you to place an order (Denver)

The Dwarf House, where the Chick-fil-A chicken sandwich was first created and served, you can still eat at this restaurant which features the original Chick-fil-A menu as well as its own diner options (Hapeville, Ga.)

Waffle House, the original location is now a museum, restored to how it looked when it first opened in 1955 (Decatur, Ga.)

Nathan's Famous, it originally began as a hot dog stand in New York's Coney Island in 1916 by Polish immigrant Nathan Handwerker, and is still in operation today (New York)

Ohio Donut Trail, visit a dozen local donut shops over 80 miles in this county that has more donut shops per capita than anywhere else in the country (Butler County, Ohio)

FOOD FESTIVALS TO ATTEND IN THE U.S.

"You are what you eat," so why not indulge in a festival devoted to one of your favorite foods? No matter what you like, there's probably a festival dedicated to it. Here's just a sampling of some of our favorites throughout the U.S. that you could add to your bucket list:

National Cherry Festival, this festival has been running annually for nearly a century, spotlighting cherries in everything from mustard to cherry pie (Traverse City, Mich.)

Maine Lobster Festival, features more than 20,000 pounds of lobster as well as fun lobster-themed events including the coronation of Marine Sea Goddess (Rockland, Maine)

Gilroy Garlic Festival, includes an array of garlic-infused foods (even garlic ice-cream!) as well as various music acts (Gilroy, Calif.)

Vermont Cheesemakers Festival, dozens of cheesemakers flock to this festival offering samples of more than 150 artisanal and farmstead cheeses (Shelbourne, Vt.)

Taste of Chicago, considered one of the biggest food festivals in the world, it draws 3 million visitors each year (Chicago)

The National Buffalo Wing Festival, the festival pays tribute to the pub mainstay that was invented here in 1964 with a wide assortment of sauces, flavors as well as the National Chicken Wing Eating Contest (Buffalo, N.Y.)

Boysenberry Food & Wine Festival, from the Knott's Berry Farm, it celebrates the boysenberry (a hybrid fruit tasting like a cross between a black-, logan- and raspberry) with more than 80 inventive foods and drinks incorporating the fruit (Buena Park, Calif.)

Cheese Curd Festival, taking place in the self-proclaimed "cheese curd capital," guests can try cheese curds in a variety of ways: fried, dipped, and even dusted in cinnamon sugar! (Ellsworth, Wis.)

SoCal Taco Fest, dozens of the area's best taco makers come for this festival that includes musical acts, chihuahua races and live traditional Mexican wrestling (San Diego)

Bluegrass & BBQ Festival, lasting over 16 days each spring, it offers a taste of BBQ from all over the country as well as more than 50 bluegrass bands (Branson, Mo.)

Cupcake Festival, it includes a pupcake pageant, a cupcake classic cruise-in and a cupcake eating contest (Hurricane, W.V.)

Blue Ribbon Bacon Festival, featuring all-things bacon, there's a bacon-eating competition and even a bacon costume contest (Des Moines, Iowa)

Cincinnati Coffee Festival, it includes coffee samplings, educational presentations and a latte art throwdown (Cincinnati)

Taste of Summer Ice Cream Festival, enjoy all-you-can ice-cream in 24 flavors during this festival that features water wars, inflatables and food trucks (Broken Arrow, Okla.)

The Great American Foodie Festival, features more than 50 of the best food trucks from around the country as well as demonstrations by celebrity chefs (Las Vegas)

The Feast of San Gennaro, celebrates Italian cuisine in New York's Little Italy as vendors line the sidewalks where you can also enter a cannoli eating contest (New York)

3-STAR RESTAURANTS FROM AROUND THE WORLD

Do you consider yourself a foodie? Then why not serve your tastebuds with the best of the best? Enter the Michelin Guide, which has been rating restaurants around the world since 1900. The highest possible rating is 3 stars. According to the guide, restaurants with this rating have "Exceptional cuisine, worth a special journey." Currently, there are about 150 restaurants around the world with a 3-star rating, but here are some to consider adding to your bucket list:

3-STAR RESTAURANTS IN THE UNITED STATES

- The Inn at Little Washington (Washington, Va.)
- Per Se (New York City)
- Le Bernardin (New York City)
- Eleven Madison Park (New York City)
- Masa (New York City)
- Smyth (Chicago)
- Alinea (Chicago)
- Atelier Crenn (San Francisco)
- Quince (San Francisco)
- Benu (San Francisco)
- Addison (San Diego)
- SingleThread Farm (Healdsburg, Calif.)
- The French Laundry (Yountville, Calif.)

3-STAR RESTAURANTS AROUND THE WORLD

- Sketch, The Lecture Room and Library (London)
- The Ledbury (London)
- Kei (Paris)
- Le Cinq (Paris)
- AM par Alexandre Mazzia (Marseille, France)
- Lasarte (Barcelona)
- DiverXO (Madrid)
- Enoteca Pinchiorri (Florence)
- Enrico Bartolini al Mudec (Milan)
- La Pergola (Rome)
- JAN (Munich)
- Rutz (Berlin)
- Memories (Bad Ragaz, Switzerland)
- Amador (Vienna, Austria)
- noma (Copenhagen)
- Maaemo (Oslo)
- Boury (Roeselare, Belgium)
- Hiša Franko (Kobarid, Slovenia)
- L'OSIER (Tokyo)
- Makimura (Tokyo)
- Mizai (Kyoto, Japan)
- Taian (Osaka, Japan)
- Ultraviolet by Paul Pairet (Shanghai)
- King's Joy (Beijing)
- Le Palais (Taiwan)
- Odette (Singapore)
- Ta Vie (Hong Kong)
- Mosu (Seoul, South Korea)

Learn more about each restaurant, their menus and what makes them special at guide.michelin.com.

ENTREPRENEURIAL ADVENTURES TO TRY

Starting your own business is not for the faint of heart. But what's a bucket list if it doesn't inspire you to go after your dreams? The same is true with your career and business goals. Here's a list of business ideas you might want to cash in on and add to your bucket list:

- Brainstorm a side-hustle
- Learn coding
- Build an app Design a logo
- Create a signature product or service
- Create a business plan
- Create a business website
- Host a pop-up shop
- Start a podcast
- Create a YouTube channel
- Start a social-media account for your business
- Attend a business conference
- Launch a crowdfunding campaign
- Get featured in the media
- Collaborate with influencers
- Appear on a podcast
- Create merch for your business
- Start a newsletter for your business
- Pitch your idea to investors
- Host an event, workshop, or webinar
- Open a physical store
- Earn $1 million dollars
- Retire early
- Be debt-free

CHARITABLE GIVING
EXPERIENCES TO DO

Research has shown that humans are wired for generosity. And for good reason: It can make us feel better, be happier and even live longer. Which is why we compiled this list of more than a dozen different ways you can give back, whether with your time or money:

- Donate blood
- Clean out your closet
- Volunteer at an animal shelter
- Learn CPR
- Send a care package to a soldier
- Start a non-profit
- Participate in a volunteer program abroad
- Perform 365 random acts of kindness
- Adopt-a-family for the holidays
- Volunteer at an animal shelter
- Participate in a wildlife conservation project
- Participate in a food, coat, or toy drive for the holidays
- Donate extra clothes to a homeless or women's shelter
- Register as an organ donor
- Grow your hair out to donate for cancer-patient wigs
- Help with a disaster-relief project
- Participate in a charity run
- Pay for a stranger's order in the car behind you
- Plant a tree on Earth Day
- Volunteer at a children's hospital
- Volunteer at a nursing home
- Volunteer at a hospice
- Volunteer at a soup kitchen
- Attend a protest

THE WORLD'S MOST SACRED SITES & SPIRITUAL EXPERIENCES FOR VARIOUS FAITHS

For nearly all of human history, religion has played an important role in people's lives. Today, about 85 percent of the world's population identify with a religion of some sort. Which means that there are loads of opportunities to delve deeper into your spirituality. We've gathered some of the most sacred practices and places for various faiths around the world for this list:

ISLAM

Great Mosque of Mecca, all Muslims pray in the direction of this holy site, considered by Muslims to be the earthly house of God (Mecca, Saudi Arabia)

Dome of the Rock, one of the oldest mosques in the world with a golden dome 177 feet high (Jerusalem)

The Blue Mosque, a still-functioning Ottoman-era mosque completed in 1619 and flanked by six minarets with elaborate, interior blue tilework (Istanbul, Turkey)

JUDAISM

Join a Shabbat dinner with a Jewish family

Attend a bar/bat mitzvah celebration

The Western Wall, also called the Wailing Wall where Jews come to pray, it is the holiest place in Judaism as the last remaining portion of the former Temple Mount platform (Jerusalem)

Mount Sinai, also called Jabal Mousa, where Moses received the Ten Commandments (Mount Sinai, Egypt)

CHRISTIANITY & CATHOLICISM

- Attend a sunrise Easter service

- Attend a candlelit Christmas Eve service

- Visit a live nativity at Christmas

- Give up something for Lent

- Pray the Stations of the Cross during Lent

- Walk a prayer labyrinth

- Go to Confessional (the Church allows this even if you aren't Catholic)

- Learn to pray the rosary

- See the Mormon Tabernacle Choir sing (Salt Lake City, Utah)

- See a gospel choir sing, such as the Mississippi Mass Choir (Jackson, Miss.) or the Brooklyn Tabernacle Choir (New York)

- **Via Dolorosa**, retrace the last steps of Jesus' leading up to his crucifixion (Jerusalem)

- **Church of the Holy Sepulchre,** believed to be the site of Jesus' tomb (Jerusalem)

- **Cathedral of Notre Dame,** which displays Jesus's Crown of Thorns, though its authenticity cannot be certified (Paris)

- **Mount of Olives**, where the Bible says Jesus ascended to heaven after his resurrection (Jerusalem)

- **The Scourging Pillars of Saints Peter and Paul,** said to be the pillars upon which both New Testament writers were tortured before their deaths (Rome)

- **The Vatican,** where you can attend a papal audience (Vatican City)

- **The Archbasilica of Saint John Lateran,** also known as the Papal church (Rome)

HINDUISM

▨ Attend a Kumbh Mela festival, the world's largest peaceful gathering of pilgrims, when they bathe in sacred rivers to free themselves from sins and the cycle of birth and death (varies, India)

▨ **Kashi Vishwanath Temple**, dedicated to the Hindu deity Shiva, it is located on the River Ganges and considered one of the most important Hindu temples (Varanasi, India)

▨ **River Ganges**, where you can take part in a Ganga Aarti ceremony every evening on the banks of the River Ganges at multiple sites (varies, India)

▨ **Sri Mariamman Temple**, built in 1827 and decorated with colorful statues of various Hindu deities, you can participate in a fire-walking ceremony (Chinatown, Singapore)

BUDDHISM

▨ **Mahabodhi Temple**, where the first Buddha supposedly achieved enlightenment (Bodh Gaya, India)

▨ **Angkor Wat**, which the *Guinness World Records* considers the largest religious structure in the world, it was originally a Hindu temple but then morphed into a Buddhist one (Siem Reap, Cambodia)

▨ **Taktsang Monastery**, it means Tiger's Nest, and is perched in the cliffs of historical Tibet (Bhutan)

▨ **Schwedagon Pagoda**, this 2,500-year-old, elaborate pagoda is festooned with gold, rubies and diamonds and is believed to house eight strands of Buddha's hair as well as other Buddhist relics (Yangon, Myanmar)

▨ **Sensoji Temple**, this five-storied pagoda with its red walls is the most-frequented spiritual site in the world and Tokyo's largest tourist attraction (Tokyo)

SHINTOISM

Ise Grand Shrine, dedicated to the sun goddess Amaterasu, its wood design is characteristic of Shinto architecture (Ise, Japan)

SIKHISM

Participate in the faith's free communal meal, known as the "langar"

Golden Temple, which sits in the middle of an artificial pond (Amritsar, India)

BAHÁ'Í FAITH

Shrine of Bahá'u'lláh, the faith's most sacred site also features the remains of the faith's founder (Acre, Israel)

INDIGENOUS AND ANCIENT SPIRITUALITY

Attend a Native American Pow Wow, which are open to the public (varies)

Uluru, also called Ayers Rock, which the local Aboriginal people believe was formed by ancestral beings during the Dreaming (Uluru, Australia)

Stonehenge, an ancient pagan site, the site is believed to be an epicenter of earth-energy (Wiltshire, England)

CELEBRATE THE HOLIDAYS

Whether it's toasting eggnog or dying Easter eggs, the holidays are perfect opportunities for forging long-lasting memories. That's why we've collected this list of festive things you can do throughout the year for your bucket list:

- Eat the traditional Southern New Year's Day meal of black-eyed peas
- Dye Easter eggs
- Hide Easter eggs for kids to discover
- Watch Fourth of July fireworks
- Host a Fourth of July grill-out
- Go apple picking
- Complete a fall corn maze
- Carve a pumpkin jack-o-lantern
- Carve a jack-o-lantern the traditional way—with a turnip!
- Visit a haunted house
- Visit a graveyard
- Dress up for Halloween
- Bake a pumpkin pie
- Host a Friendsgiving meal
- Roast a turkey
- Decorate a Christmas tree
- Design and send holiday cards (even if they're just you!)
- Bake Christmas cookies
- Make a gingerbread house
- Create homemade gifts for the holidays
- Sit in front of a fireplace
- Build a winter bonfire

- Drink hot cocoa
- Drink eggnog
- Make a snow angel
- Go sledding
- Build a snowman
- Build a snow fort or igloo
- Make snow cones or snow ice-cream
- Create a snow obstacle course
- Make a snow volcano or snow candle
- See an ice-sculpture
- Brainstorm New Year resolutions
- Stay up for a New Year's Eve countdown (see list, p. 104)

THE MOST UNIQUE NEW YEAR'S EVE BALL DROPS AROUND THE U.S.

While the iconic Times Square ball drop in New York City is the most well-known New Year's Eve celebration, lots of other places around the country have put their own spin on this iconic event: We've rounded up the most quirky and unusual "ball drops" we could find—because why not start the new year off with a bang—or, perhaps, a pickle?!

Possum Drop, a taxidermied possum named Spencer is lowered from a pole at the stroke of midnight (Tallapoosa, Georgia)

Flea Drop, this giant, 30-lb. flea named "Langston" is a nod to the area's history of cotton farming (Eastover, N.C.)

Peach Drop, an 800-pound fiberglass peach drops from a 138-foot tower of lights (Atlanta)

Beach Ball Drop, a huge, glowing beach ball is lowered amid a firework display (Panama City Beach, Fla.)

Glowing Pickle Drop, the pickle company named for the town lowers a giant pickle into a giant pickle jar at midnight (Mount Olive, N.C.)

Taco Drop, Taco Bell lowers a giant glowing taco amid a firework display (Tucson, Ariz.)

Idaho Potato Drop, a giant, flowing artificial potato, dubbed the GlowTato, falls at midnight (Boise, Idaho)

Acorn Drop, a 10-foot-tall copper and steel acorn was commissioned for the city's bicentennial and has been lowered on NYE every year since (Raleigh, N.C.)

Bologna Drop, pays tribute to the town's production of the luncheon meat during the 19th century (Lebanon, Pa.)

WHAT'S ON YOUR BUCKET LIST?

LEAVE A *Review*

BRING YOUR BUCKET LIST TO LIFE WITH THE COMPANION PLANNING JOURNAL!

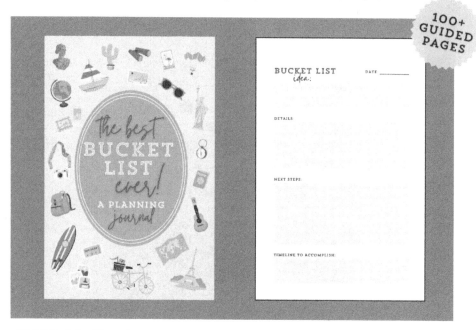

100+ GUIDED PAGES

TURN YOUR DREAMS INTO REALITY!

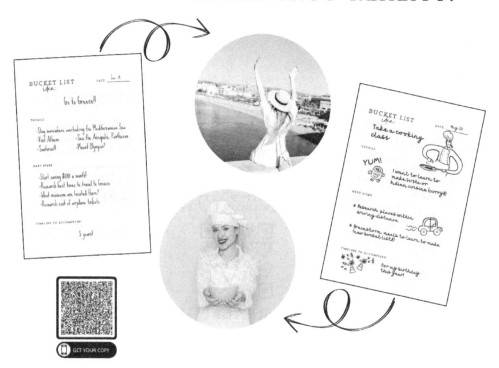

CREATE YOUR OWN BUCKET LIST

Add your own bucket list ideas here!

_____

_____

_____

_____

_____

_____

_____

_____

_____

_____

_____

_____

_____

_____

Made in the USA
Middletown, DE
21 December 2024